To S. M. P., with love —D. E.

Copyright © 2008 by Dilys Evans.
All rights reserved.
Image copyright and credit information on page 145.

Book design by Sara Gillingham.
Typeset in Andrade Pro and Gotham.
Manufactured in China.

Library of Congress Cataloging-in-Publication Data
Evans, Dilys.
Show and tell : exploring the fine art of children's book illustration / by Dilys Evans.
p. cm.
ISBN: 978-0-8118-4971-5
1. Illustrated children's books—United States—History—21st century. 2. Illustrators—
United States. I. Title.
NC975.E93 2008
741.6'42092273—dc22
2006027981

10 9 8 7 6 5 4 3 2 1

Chronicle Books LLC
680 Second Street, San Francisco, California 94107

www.chroniclekids.com

DILYS EVANS

# SHOW & TELL

## EXPLORING THE FINE ART OF CHILDREN'S BOOK ILLUSTRATION

chronicle books · san francisco

# AUTHOR'S NOTE

The tradition of show-and-tell has been with us for a very long time. Some of the earliest examples can be found on the walls of prehistoric caves. The role of cave paintings was to vividly re-create the story of the hunt—not just to show the details of a specific event but to help the audience feel the powerful emotions of the hunt and to inspire them to go out and hunt again.

Imagine the artist patiently searching the cave's walls for just the right spot. And, on finding a small mound of stone rising slightly from the surface, realizing that there hidden from the eyes of others, the image has already begun. With a sweeping arc of charcoal a large bison emerges from the stone, no longer a flat image but a three-dimensional beast ready to leap right off the wall.

When I look at children's book illustration, I often find myself thinking about the cave painter who saw that bump in the wall, and I look for that same kind of artistic vision that both shows and tells the story.

All these thousands of years later, the purpose of the picture and the process of creating it are much the same. The materials may have changed, but human instincts have stayed pretty much the same. Every illustrator uses his imagination, looks for the best surface to work upon and the right tools for the job. The best illustrators feel the sheer power of line, imagine the precise moment, smell the air and feel breeze. And when they feel it, we the viewer share those moments.

It turns out that the leap from the very best of cave art to the very best of children's book art is but a hiccup in time.

The definition of "art" has been debated for centuries, but to my mind art happens when a particular creation stops us in our tracks. It makes us think. It touches our deepest emotions and oftentimes it teaches us something new.

Historically, children's picture books have not been categorized as fine art. Even a mere twenty-five years ago this was a relatively new concept, and the very reason I used the term to describe the first Original Art Exhibition at the Master Eagle Gallery in New York. The term "fine art" as we knew it then automatically assumed paintings and sculptures in galleries or museums. My mission in organizing that first exhibition in 1980 was to create an awareness that children's book illustration was a unique form of fine art that was worthy of celebration and recognition.

My goal in this book is to explore some of the very best picture books that qualify for that distinction. As part of this exploration I looked for powerful imagery and storytelling ability that goes beyond a simple interpretation of the text or event. I looked for illustrators who find that bump in the wall and bring the character right off the page and into my lap.

For my purposes I needed a wide range of styles, techniques, and content. Some of the illustrators I have chosen are icons in the children's book world, others are relative newcomers. But this is not a "best of" list. That would be impossible, given the incredible number of talented artists working in children's books today. These are all artists whose work I admire. But they are not the only artists whose work I admire. And I could just have easily chosen twelve different artists to show and tell the story of the fine art of children's book illustration. My purpose was not to profile a particular group of illustrators but to choose a group that would offer readers as broad a frame of reference as possible.

Ultimately, my hope is that this book might help all of us who value children's books to find a universal language to use to talk about art on the page; a vocabulary that helps describe this unique form of artistic expression with greater clarity and common understanding. And that we will then take that vocabulary and use it to explore the many other wonderful books that are on our shelves.

In this regard, we truly suffer from an embarrassment of riches. Children's books have never looked better or been more important. They are one of the few quiet places left where a child can go to be alone, and to travel worlds past, present, and future. They are often the first place children dis-cover poetry and art, honor and loyalty, right and wrong, sadness and hope. And it is there between the pages that children discover the power of their own imaginations. They are indeed a dress rehearsal for life.

# TABLE OF CONTENTS

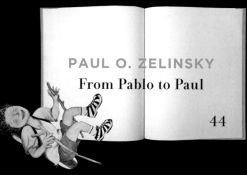
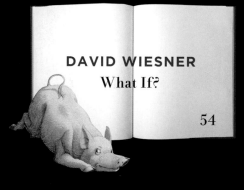

# HILARY KNIGHT
## A Natural Born Rascal

If you ask Hilary Knight when he decided to become an artist, he'll tell you, *"I never thought I would be anything else."*

Born in 1926 in Hempstead, Long Island, Knight grew up in a wonderful old house just a few yards from the Roslyn public library, where he spent many hours. Both his parents were successful commercial and book illustrators, so Knight grew up in an atmosphere where picture making was a part of everyday life.

His mother, Katharine Sturges, was originally from Chicago, and when she was just eighteen she traveled to Japan to study Oriental art. In 1917, that was a remarkably bold adventure for such a young woman. She was to become well known in the worlds of both commercial and fashion illustration for her graceful curvilinear style and a lavish use of birds and flowers in the tradition of Oriental art. Knight's father, Clayton Knight, was an immensely popular aviation illustrator. In fact, when Hilary Knight was born, his father named him after a famous French aviator.

Knight's father traveled into the city each day to work in his studio. Knight's mother had a small studio on the top floor of their house, with views out the dormer windows. She created very large oil paintings for magazine illustrations, which to the young Knight seemed to fill the room. He too worked at home, with the paper, pencils, and crayons his mother gave him.

It was a tremendously exciting time for a young artist to grow up. The 1920s and '30s were the golden years for the art of illustration. It was the era of the glossy magazine, which became a showcase for some of the most prestigious names in the graphic arts. Artists such as N. C. Wyeth, Jessie Willcox Smith, Elizabeth Shippen Green, Norman Rockwell, Boris Artzybasheff, Pruett A. Carter, John La Gatta, Dean Cornwell, and the Leyendecker brothers were all a part of this incredibly creative and productive time.

Photography was just a fledgling art form, only beginning to realize its enormous potential in the magazine world. Meanwhile, publications like *Harper's Bazaar*, the *Saturday Evening Post*, *Ladies' Home Journal*, the *New Yorker*, and *St. Nicholas* magazine for children were all employing illustrators to create full-color jacket art and black-and-white interiors. Advertising agencies, which had recently arrived on the scene, were a powerful influence on the graphic persona of the time.

Knight's home was a gathering place for family, friends, and other artists. There was constant talk, laughter, and the sharing of ideas accompanied by good food and wine. "Even the grown-ups seemed to have fun," he recalls. Knight's mother loved the Art Deco style, and much of the house was decorated in beautiful fabrics with geometric designs and bright colors. There were always elegant vases and flowers, Oriental scrolls, and of course paintings. It's not surprising that these flamboyant surroundings would one day become the wellspring of Knight's unique high style and wicked humor. To this day he maintains that his parents were the most important influences on his work.

As a boy, Knight spent hours looking at books that belonged to his mother. He would forever be fascinated by the humorous illustrations of Boutet de Monvel, the haunting beauty, romance, and fantasy of Edmund Dulac's work, and the sophisticated designs of both artists. It was, however, Winnie-the-Pooh who garnered first place in his heart. A. A. Milne's classic was first published in October 1926, the year Knight was born, and he (like many children since then) grew up with Christopher Robin, Pooh, Piglet, Eeyore, Kanga, baby Roo, and of course, Tigger.

"Ernest Shepard was truly remarkable. His black-and-white pen-and-ink technique is so simple and direct. Edmund Dulac, on the other hand, was sheer fantasy. He was so glamorous and exotic. He went from very elaborate and painterly watercolors to completely stylized Persian paintings. His work is so extraordinary and I love the exoticism of it."

Knight's family shared many outings to the beach, the theater, and of course, the circus, which proved to be a magical place for Knight. This exposure to the performing arts left a lasting impression on him, setting the stage, as it were, for his career as a children's book illustrator.

Knight also loved listening to the radio and was passionate about movies. He first saw *The Wizard of Oz* in 1939, and remembers it as a truly magical night in the quiet of a darkened movie theater. The lush color, the scale of the pictures, and the romantic theatricality of it all made a pivotal impression. And when he finally began making his own pictures for children's books, that particular movie often played an unconscious part in his creative process.

While it's true that Knight was always interested in books and art as a child, he was by no means sedentary. Looking at old black-and-white movies of the family during their summer vacations at the shore, whenever young Hilary is glimpsed, he is dashing madly about.

In 1932, when Knight was six years old, the family moved to Greenwich Village in New York City, and Knight was enrolled at the City & Country School. From there he went to the High School for Music and Art, but the formality of the school did not fit his free spirit, so when he was fourteen he moved to the Friends Seminary. At sixteen his mother let him enroll at the Art Students League to study art. Finally he felt at home. He started making jewelry, and for the next two years he designed and crafted many beautiful pieces that his mother's friends were anxious to buy.

Of all the teachers at the Art Students League, Reginald Marsh stands out as the teacher who truly understood the needs of this high-spirited young student. He constantly challenged Knight to work hard and expand his thinking about the "art" of drawing. "Reginald Marsh really taught me how to draw, how to see the figure . . . and construct it, and that drawing does not necessarily mean being anatomically exact."

Knight also admired the paintings and drawings of John Singer Sargent, and from a very early age he loved Degas. However, he was particularly fascinated with the powerfully moody and energetic black line work of George Bellows.

At the age of eighteen, with World War II raging, Knight joined the Navy. After an eighteen-month tour of duty, he returned home to New York and decided to become a set designer. He studied drafting, and eventually had the opportunity to become an assistant stage manager for a summer stock theater company in Ogunquit, Maine. There he fell in love with theater for life. He loved creating the scenery and working with large backgrounds of color. However, the scale of the work and the fact that decisions made by so many other people affected his designs did not sit well with this independent young man. He then went on to meet and work for James Astor, a decorator.

"This was a truly wonderful time for me. I did a lot of drawings of designed interiors and learned a lot of different things there, including fabric design."

At about the same time, he began reading *Punch* and *Lilliput* magazines—both British publications full of drawings by some of the best English illustrators of the 1950s, including Ronald Searle, Norman Thelwell, and Heath Robinson. Many of the drawings were vigorous and full of wicked good humor, which made an instant connection with this young American artist looking for his next step forward. *Hurrah for St. Trinians*, written and illustrated by Ronald Searle and published in London in 1948, was a particular favorite. He loved the action and madcap humor of *St. Trinians*, set in an English boarding school for high-spirited young girls. The art was realized in strong, energetic black line—Knight's favorite technique.

In the early 1950s Knight took his portfolio to *Mademoiselle* magazine. The art director at the time, Leo Lerman, loved Knight's black line work, especially the drawings of schoolgirls in the tradition of Ronald Searle. Soon Knight began getting assignments from *House & Garden* and *Gourmet* magazine as well, and the latter allowed him to work in two-color illustration instead of black-and-white. As part of creating pages for fashion magazines, he found himself drawing children in all kinds of situations and backgrounds. Then one day D. D. Dixon of *Harper's Bazaar* introduced him to Kay Thompson, the talented singer and supper-club entertainer.

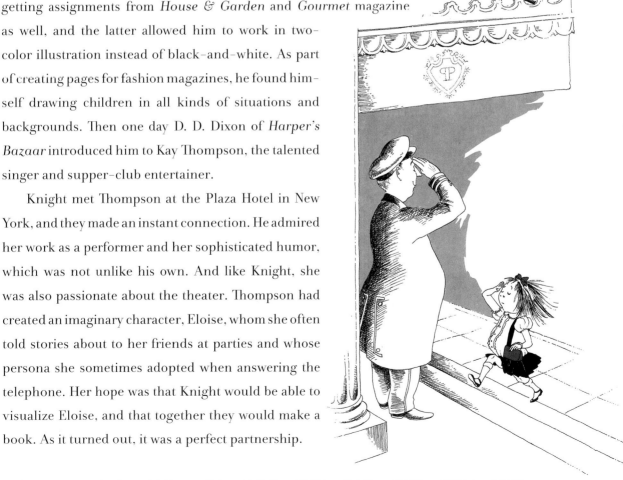

Knight met Thompson at the Plaza Hotel in New York, and they made an instant connection. He admired her work as a performer and her sophisticated humor, which was not unlike his own. And like Knight, she was also passionate about the theater. Thompson had created an imaginary character, Eloise, whom she often told stories about to her friends at parties and whose persona she sometimes adopted when answering the telephone. Her hope was that Knight would be able to visualize Eloise, and that together they would make a book. As it turned out, it was a perfect partnership.

The whimsical energy of Hilary Knight's black line work was the perfect complement to the frantic fun displayed by Eloise. The delicate curvilinear touches that conveyed the elegance of the Plaza Hotel came straight from his memories of his childhood and from Oriental art.

The book, published in 1955, was pre-separated, using black ink with pen to create the drawings, and a bright red for the overlay. After completing the drawings on double-faced Strathmore board, he then shaded the areas on the overlays made of acetate that would be printed as the second color, red. Cross-hatching created shading and volume, and solid black or red emphasized areas of importance.

The main characteristic that runs throughout Knight's work is his impeccable sense of theater. He doesn't merely create pictures, he presents them to us. Many of his books have borders of one sort or another, and often these borders have a specific role. Like a stage, they both contain and present the scene.

In *Eloise*, the choice of a vertical format is all-important, since it gives the illustrations of the Plaza Hotel a grand, upright scale. The hallways and sumptuous gathering spaces have a feeling of luxury and elegance. And the relatively small bustling figure of Eloise has a vast stage to roam. She is clearly the star, and she directs the action, which begins immediately on the book's front cover.

Eloise is highly visible in her solid black skirt and shoes, crisp white blouse, and red bow in her hair. Her back is to the world as she climbs up the front of a marble fireplace to write the name *Eloise*, the book's title, in the mirror. At the bottom of the fireplace, a small black rectangle of carpet invites us into the scene. Opening the book, there she is again—on the front flap in three different and commanding poses. She then proceeds to dash off the right-hand endpaper into the title page. The angularity of her body, hair streaming out behind her, and the cross-hatching of her shadow all direct her forward motion, and the pace is set to portray the extraordinary high energy of this child.

Throughout the book one sees the importance of the line. It curves to suggest coziness or femininity, it becomes angular to convey motion or danger. At the same time, the line establishes clear areas of positive white space, which play a large role in the artist's overall design.

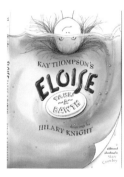

Anatomically speaking, these drawings are not perfect. Instead they capture the personality so crucial to creating believable characters. Weenie, Eloise's beloved pug; the wiry energy of the skinny bellboys; the plump good cheer of the governess—each owe their strong presence to Knight's ability to render speed, humor, and chaos, all at the same time.

Following up on the phenomenal success of the first book, *Eloise in Paris* was published in 1957 and *Eloise at Christmastime* in 1958. *Eloise in Moscow* came in 1959. Knight had spent four weeks in Moscow and Leningrad doing research for the book. Unprepared for the classic beauty and grandeur of the architecture, Knight was truly inspired. He still believes that *Eloise in Moscow* contains some of his very best work in the series.

The final book in the series, *Eloise Takes a Bawth*, was published in 2002, after Kay Thompson's death.

Knight went on to write children's books himself and to illustrate many written by others. To date, he has worked on over eighty books for children. And while his work in the Eloise books may be his most widely recognized, he has produced numerous other titles that have showcased his remarkable technical skill and originality.

While Knight is best known for his energetic line, fresh color, and meticulous attention to the technical aspects of his drawing, his art can also simply be warm, cozy, and funny, not unlike Garth Williams.

# ELOISE IN MOSCOW

## The Author Speaks Freely

FOUND RUSSIA
**"BIG BIG BIG"**

NEW YORK, 1959 – "It looked like a medieval Buffalo, New York," says Kay Thompson, just back from her groundbreaking trip to Moscow. Miss Thompson, the world-renowned performer, author, and trendsetter, now adds "diplomat" to her titles.

Miss Thompson explains how she and illustrator Hilary Knight found themselves in Communist territory: "Art Buchwald said, 'Kay, you have to go to Moscow,' and I said, 'Fine,'" she recalls. "I called Hilary and said, 'Let's be tourists and go to Russia!' and he said, 'Fine.'"

The Iron Curtain fell for Thompson and her entourage.

*Continued on back page*

## The Beatles Twist and Shout

FAB FOUR SEND
A TELEGRAM

LIVERPOOL, ENGLAND, 1964
DEAR ELOISE. WE WISH WE COULD HOLD YOUR HAND. YEAH, YEAH, YEAH.
—THE BEATLES

*Drawings By*
## HILARY KNIGHT

## The Artist's Diary Unlocked for First Time

"WE SUBSISTED ON
BORSCHT AND CAVIAR"

*Following are excerpts from the recently rediscovered diary of Hilary Knight. An Eloise exclusive.*

NEW YORK – MOSCOW – NEW YORK, February 19 to March 26, 1959 – We're off in style. A gray Rolls-Royce whips us to Idlewild Airport as Kay's sister, Blanche, waves goodbye. . . . Kay's luggage includes daywear, evening wear, furs, fezzes, muffs (ear and hand); mine, pads, paints & pencils. We're ready for anything.

Into Paris and jet to Moscow. . . . Aida, our Intourist guide, delivers us to the Hotel Ukraine, Moscow's pride. . . . It's a charmless marble mausoleum in a town painted shades of ochre & mustard. "Eloise can't stay here," insists Kay. "We must move!" Aida states: "IS NOT POSSIBLE. TO MOVE HOTELS YOU MUST LEAVE MOSCOW AND RE-ENTER." This we did.

Side trip to Leningrad then back to Moscow and a hotel with nothing

*Continued on back page*

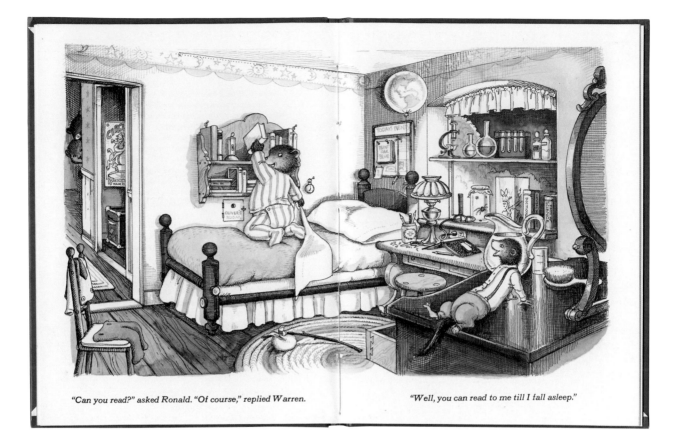

"Can you read?" asked Ronald. "Of course," replied Warren.

"Well, you can read to me till I fall asleep."

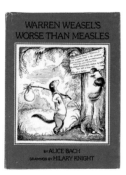

Knight's work in *Warren Weasel's Worse Than Measles*, written by Alice Bach and published in 1980, is an example of black-and-white art at its very best. The story is about a young weasel looking for his place in the world and a young bear looking for friendship. In one picture, Ronald Bear is looking for a book for Warren to read to him. This bedroom setting perfectly suits the little scientist bear, with a workbench dresser and a line of test tubes on the top shelf next to a microscope, alchemy jars, and glass bottles. **The magic here is Knight's ability to express a beginning friendship, the warmth of a cozy bedroom, and the feeling of being safe at home—all without the use of color.** The eye contact between the two animals is expressive, and the room is full of curves, the most comforting of linear expressions. Through the open door, both parents can be seen peeking in from the end of the hallway, and there on a side wall is a scrap of a poster advertising a circus. Cross-hatching and a dark gray wash give the room a cozy feeling, and on top of a chest of drawers we find Warren leaning back on his paws, waiting expectantly for the book he will read out loud to his friend tonight. With its full range of tonality and linear strength, this picture is a painting that tells a story.

Knight's love of romance and decoration are most evident in another title, *Beauty and the Beast*, published in 1963. The art in this book is influenced by the flamboyant forms of Art Nouveau and is illustrated in rich, fresh color. Here his childhood memories of his mother's decorative flair have found their home.

But for sheer theater and technical wizardry, we must turn to *The Circus Is Coming*. Originally published in 1978, Knight created all new illustrations for an updated version published in 2007. The double-page spread below presents fun, action, and—of course—forward motion as the parade moves steadily throughout the book. The color here is bright and powerful in shades of green, yellow, and orange-red, and it's interesting to note that he uses the white space actively to keep the entire form moving in space. Once again the white background doesn't merely present the art, it also helps create the feeling of constant motion across the pages.

The main character here is the Fire Dragon, an exciting and friendly looking fellow, who seems to be very actively involved in the moment. The performers fly, juggle, or tumble forward, and a little girl flying through the hoop makes eye contact with a small boy passing by (does she remind us of someone?). Again, a horizontal line at the bottom of the page acts like a stage. A boy seems to be going the wrong way—or is he? Naturally our eye follows the action and we just have to turn the page.

From China! A tumbling troupe that twirls, twists, and turns!

In *Side by Side*, an anthology of poems collected by Lee Bennett Hopkins and published in 1988, readers can find another example of Knight's love of theater and design in a full-color illustration he did for "Seven Little Rabbits" by John Becker.

The cutaway view of Mole's hole shows us seven little rabbits tucked snugly into Mole's bed, which is constructed in the style of pure "Twig" Art Deco. Across the gutter, Mole and Frog are having tea and a piece of carrot cake.

Meanwhile Mrs. Rabbit is above ground, looking down into the cozy scene, the night sky around her. The separation between the two worlds is achieved by Knight's use of the grass, which is painted into a proscenium-like border. Once again each animal has a unique expression that gives us a clue to that particular animal's feelings. Like Beatrix Potter, Knight has the ability to create animal characters that seem real to the reader and are not overly sweet or cute.

To Knight, the most exciting part about doing any book is the planning. He loves working out the thumbnails, pacing the pages so the story remains in constant motion, and thinking through the execution. He then goes straight to putting finishes on the "working sketches," which then become the actual finished art.

"I like to work on double-faced Strathmore board so that it can be peeled for the scanner, and I use ordinary watercolor, pencil, and pen—nothing fancy.

*One* little rabbit
Walkin' down the road
Walkin' down the road
One little rabbit
Walkin' down the road
To call on old friend toad.

One little rabbit
Said he was tired
Walkin' down the road
Walkin' down the road
One little rabbit
Said he was tired
Walkin' down the road
To call on old friend toad.

So
One little rabbit
Turned around
Until he found
Down in the ground
A hole
Built by a mole.

❖ 44 ❖

"Working this way, I hope to keep the spontaneity and freshness in each picture. It should never look tired or overworked. I don't like the idea of working over the lines of a sketch; it kills the life of the thing for me."

When I asked Knight who some of his favorite children's book illustrators are, he named Chris van Allsburg, Maurice Sendak, and Ian Falconer. It's interesting to note that all three of these artists have had extensive involvement with the theater.

After the death of Kay Thompson in 1998, Simon & Schuster approached her estate for permission to reprint the three Eloise books that she had withdrawn from publication (*Paris*, *Christmastime*, and *Moscow*). Permission was given, and all three books were very quickly back in print and in great demand. Soon after the return of Eloise, Simon & Schuster located the other Hilary Knight titles they owned, and brought *The Twelve Days of Christmas* and *The Owl and the Pussy-cat* back into print as well. Knight is enjoying this renaissance, and continues to work on books from both his Long Island studio and his studio in New York City, which he shares with his vivacious black Persian cat, Ruff II, who runs both households and is, of course, a natural born rascal.

The one little rabbit
Went down the hole
Built by the mole
Down in the ground
Until he found
A den.

*Then*
The first little rabbit
Who was also the last
Went to sleep—
Now don't say "Peep"—
He's tucked in bed
And now instead
Of walkin' down the road
Of walkin' down the road

The first little rabbit
Dreamed a dream
And to him it seemed
All in a blur
As if there were

Seven little rabbits
Walkin' down the road
Walkin' down the road
Seven little rabbits
Walkin' down the road
To call on old friend toad.

JOHN BECKER

❖ 45 ❖

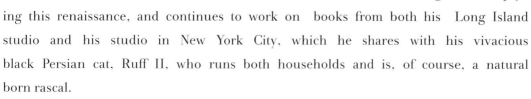

# TRINA SCHART HYMAN
## Little Red

"My mother read to me from the time I was a baby. Once, when I was three or four and she was reading my favorite story, the words on the page, her spoken words, and the scenes in my head fell together in a blinding flash. I could read! The story was *Little Red Riding Hood*, and it became so much a part of me that I *became* Little Red Riding Hood."

When Hyman was a little girl, her mother made her a red satin cape with a hood. Hyman wore it almost every day for a whole year and acted out the story in her garden, with Tippy the dog playing the part of the wolf and her father the part of the kindly woods-man returning home every night from work. A great many children play imaginary games and become different characters in their young lives, but it's rare that a performance lasts 365 days. That's exactly the kind of singular passion Hyman has always brought to the drawing table. Her characters are memorable, and we the viewers are given powerful por-traits that make lasting impressions.

As a very young child Hyman was timid and terrified of everything, especially people and other children.

"As a kid I liked to hide under the table and under bushes, look at pictures, and read books; [I'd] lie on my back and look at the ceiling and imagine what it would be like if I could walk on the ceiling. I liked to lie on my stomach in the grass and think what it would be like if I were [so] tiny that the grass would be a forest. I played a lot of imaginary games. I liked to play by myself best, or with one other person. I didn't like to play with groups of kids until I was about seven or eight."

Born in Pennsylvania in 1939, Hyman grew up north of Philadelphia in a rural area. She lived across the road from a large working farm. The farm was run by a caretaker who had two daughters. Hyman and the youngest daughter became good friends, playing together for hours. Hyman also always had an affinity for all kinds of animals, so being able to play on the farm seemed like a dream come true.

From the time she could hold a pencil, Hyman made art. By the time she was twelve years old, she realized there were people who painted pictures for a living, and in junior high school she discovered book illustration. She knew immediately this was what she desperately wanted to do.

As a child, Hyman's mother read to her constantly, and though the stories were always intriguing, the pictures were what really made an impact. Of Jessie Willcox Smith's illustrations for *A Child's Garden of Verses* by Robert Louis Stevenson, she said simply, "I loved those pictures . . . you could live in them."

Other firm favorites were *Grimm's Fairy Tales*, illustrated in black-and-white by Fritz Kredel; *The Merry Adventures of Robin Hood* and *The Wonder Clock* by Howard Pyle; and *Dreadful Hollow* by Irena Karlova, a book about vampires, demons, and all the really scary stuff that Hyman relished in high school. Nancy Drew was also a passion, read many times over, and *Little Red Riding Hood* still kept her place on this notable list.

By the time Hyman was a senior in high school she was determined to be an artist. Her parents were very supportive of her decision, and she was able to enroll in a special life-drawing class for high-school students at the Philadelphia Museum of Fine Art.

"Every Saturday, my father would drive me into Philadelphia and then pick me up at the end of class. He was fantastic. And imagine three whole hours of life drawing. I knew then that I belonged in that place and that was where I wanted to be. I didn't even bother to apply to any other art school. Luckily I managed to get a full scholarship, and that was a great beginning."

The Philadelphia Museum of Fine Art had a fine reputation as a commercial art school. The faculty at that time was impressive and was led by Henry C. Pitz, head of the illustration department. He was also an author who went on to write *The Brandywine Tradition*, considered the definitive book on Brandywine artists, including N. C. Wyeth, Howard Pyle, and Jessie Willcox Smith. Hyman loved the work of these artists. As it happened, Henry Pitz liked Hyman's work as well as her fiery enthusiasm, and he encouraged her to realize her dream. She credits him with her decision to become a children's book illustrator.

It was also during this time that Hyman discovered Pennsylvania German Fraktur painting. It was her first connection with folk art of any kind, and she loved it. She worked it into her school projects and spent hours imitating it to better understand it. Fraktur painting possessed qualities found in medieval illustrated manuscripts, with its elegant hand lettering and glowing color. Looking at the border designs in many of her picture books, together with the hand lettering of some of her book titles, we can see its influence.

Once dedicated to her career of choice, Hyman began taking her portfolio to publishing houses in Philadelphia, Boston, and New York, and started receiving enthusiastic encouragement. By the time she was a sophomore in college she had several assignments from children's educational publishers.

When she was twenty-one she left art school in order to marry Harris Hyman, a mechanical engineer who had just gotten a job in Boston. She attended the School of the Museum of Fine Arts in Boston for a year, but her husband then received a scholarship to study at the University of Stockholm, so it was off to Sweden. Hyman once again enrolled in art school, and again she took her portfolio around to publishers. This time, she landed her first real job illustrating a children's book.

The name of the publisher was Rabén & Sjögren, a major Swedish publisher, and the children's book editor who admired her work was none other than Astrid Lindgren. Lindgren was also well known as the author of the Pippi Longstocking books.

"I was ecstatic! It was a chapter book for third or fourth graders with forty-six black-and-white line drawings. It took me about three months to translate the story from Swedish to English, and a matter of weeks to do the actual work in black-line. I was paid the equivalent of three hundred dollars, and I was now a published illustrator."

Hyman used the three hundred dollars to buy a bright blue tandem bicycle, and she and her husband decided to take a bicycle trip. They rode across Sweden to Denmark, and then up Denmark and across Norway. The final leg of their trip took them across England and Scotland. They bicycled a total of three thousand miles in three months.

Bicycling through the huge dark forests and lush valleys of the Nordic countryside was a life-changing experience. At night the pure darkness and scale created unique memories that would inspire and nourish her imagination for years to come.

"Those beech forests with no undergrowth whatsoever, just the big old silent trees, were magical, and there's an ancient wildness to the nature in Scandinavia that you don't get anywhere else. I also really loved the north of England and the Yorkshire dales and moors—so different and wonderful."

On returning to Boston, Hyman longed to illustrate fairy and folk tales and wanted to work for an established publisher. Her decision to revisit Little, Brown and Company would prove to be the answer to her dreams. Helen Jones, the children's book editor at that time, really understood what this fiery and ambitious young artist was all about.

"That was the start of the most important relationship of my professional life and an important friendship, as well. Every young artist needs a special someone—a teacher, a friend, or an editor who will say, 'I believe in you.'"

Hyman's very first books with Helen Jones were *Joy to the World* by Ruth Sawyer, a book of Christmas stories and poems, and *Favorite Tales Told in Czechoslovakia*, retold by Virginia Haviland.

In 1963, Hyman's daughter Katrin was born. It was a very happy time. The Hymans were living in their own little house that was constantly full of friends and stray cats—and a growing collection of beloved pet mice. There were lots of parties and bike rides out into the country. But intermingled with the joy was sadness for Hyman, who really longed for a house in the countryside. But that was not to be. Instead they moved to New York for her husband's next job. It turned out to be a bad move for everyone. Hyman felt imprisoned by the city, eventually the marriage collapsed, and she and Katrin left New York for life in a big, old stone house in Lyme, New Hampshire.

Not long after the move to Lyme, Marianne and Blouke Carus, a couple from Chicago, came to talk to Hyman about becoming the art director for a new children's magazine by the name of *Cricket*. Hyman said yes, and for the first time in her life she had a steady income, and with the promise of more manuscripts to come from Little, Brown, she felt secure.

It was for Little, Brown that Hyman wrote a story called *How Six Found Christmas*, published in 1969. She was now an author as well as an illustrator. Then came the turning point in her career: a book titled *King Stork* by Howard Pyle, one of her heroes. Although she was not well known enough to be given a full-color book commission, she illustrated it with four-color separations.

The original black-line drawing was reproduced on one printing plate and each of the other colors were printed on separate plates. By lining up these plates one directly above the other, the final printing produced a "full-color" image. Hyman used four acetate sheets, one for each color, and she registered the lined-up pages herself so the images would print perfectly. Fortunately this archaic way of printing is now a thing of the past.

The overall design and use of color in this book was magical, and despite the laborious process, her drawing appeared effortless. Published by Little, Brown and Company in 1973, *King Stork* garnered the Boston Globe–Horn Book Award. It also got the attention of Emily McLeod, the children's book editor at Atlantic Monthly Press in Boston, who called Hyman and asked what she would most like to illustrate next.

Hyman met with McLeod and made an instant connection, and so *Snow White*, retold by Paul Heins, came to be illustrated in full, glowing color. This book was proof of Hyman's extraordinary skills in drawing and dramatic composition. It also showcased her unique ability to handle color and light.

Most of the great moments of high drama in the story occur at night. Establishing a light source was critical in dark scenes, where just the action needed to be featured. Hyman found that if she mixed glazes—color varnishes that add a richness and glow to the color beneath—with her color for the dark scenes, the color kept more of its life.

She hand lettered both the cover art and the title pages, and the overall design of this book is classic in its execution.

In the scene shown here, we see Snow White after she's been running wildly through the forest. She is completely alone, terrified of everything around her while the daylight fades and she looks for a safe place to hide. The sense of place created here is tangible. A fading orange-cream sky, filtering through the forest, backlights the trees in the distance. In the forest is a small woodsman's cottage, complete with a fieldstone chimney, a barrel for collecting water, and an ax left in the chopping block, its blade catching a glint of evening light. A cozy yellow glow spills from the window onto a spot next to the

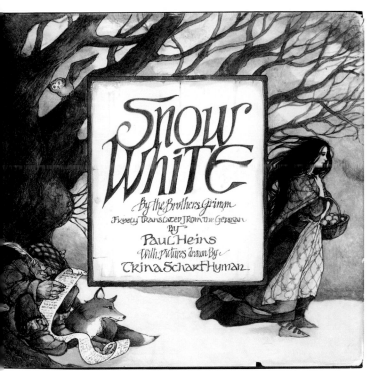

Now the poor child was completely alone in the great forest. She was frightened and did not know what to do. She began to run, and stumbled over sharp stones and into thorns. Wild animals sprang past her, but did her no harm. She ran as long as her legs could carry her until just before evening when she saw a little house and went inside to rest. In the house, everything was small, but neat and clean. There stood a little table, spread with a white cloth and laid with seven small plates, seven small spoons, seven little knives and forks, and seven little goblets. Against the wall were seven small beds placed in a row, and covered with white spreads. So hungry and thirsty was Snow White that she ate a bit of vegetable and a bit of bread from each plate, and drank a sip of wine from each goblet; for she did not want to take everything away from any one place. Afterward, since she was very tired, she tried lying down on one of the little beds, but none of them satisfied her—one was too long, another too short—until finally the seventh one seemed to be just right. There she stayed, said her prayers, and fell asleep.

rain barrel, a welcoming sign for the frightened young girl. Everything is orderly and calls out that all is well and safe. Like Snow White, we the viewers can gradually relax a little, too.

Just off center is Snow White—a truly beautiful child—her left hand clutching her shawl about her shoulders while her right hand rests on the trunk of a large tree. All the jewel-like color and light is focused here to create a vivid contrast with the darkness behind her in the forest. Her fear is palpable—exactly what the text demands. There is a strange paleness to her skin, and her eyes are wide. Her long black hair curls about her face and shoulders and is wild in the wind—can you hear it? The tree trunk is perfectly centered across the gutter and spreads to the right-hand page, creating a separation between the past terror of the dark woods and this turning point in the story. Those three thousand miles Hyman rode through the forests of Europe, coupled with her life in New England, come together in this painting.

This particular image truly demonstrates how to paint an emotion. Imagination is key here, and Hyman is known to have much more than her fair share.

"If you can't imagine yourself [in] every single character's skin, and if you can't imagine yourself into the landscape of the book or [feel] what it feels like to be a rain-soaked and battle-scarred hero—if you can't imagine it, you can't feel it. And if you can't feel it, you can't put the energy of it into your picture, so you've lost your connection with the reader and you are just doing decoration!"

As one book now followed another, it was an old friend who helped Hyman finally capture the attention of the prestigious Caldecott Committee: *Little Red Riding Hood*, which she both retold and illustrated, earned her the 1984 Caldecott Honor.

In the image shown here, we have an entirely different mood. This moment calls for sunshine and light, a sense of home and safety, and the feeling of the woods in springtime. It is therefore all the more shocking when the bad wolf enters the story.

The hand lettering and decorative border are reminiscent of both primitive painting and Fraktur, with its beautiful calligraphy and decorative simplicity. The full-color frontispiece on the left is a wonderful welcome to the story, while the title page on the right is a perfect example of what can be done to make an otherwise ordinary page spectacular.

Created with pencil and acrylic paint, the picture shows Little Red Riding Hood sitting on a bench outside her front door and reading a book. Next to her is a contented-looking white cat, and down on the ground beside her is her favorite black cat, who will stay at her side throughout the story. Eventually it will be the black cat that goes for help when Little Red needs it most, and even in this tranquil scene, this cat is clearly on alert.

The little white clapboard house looks cozy. Through the open door, we see Little Red's mother working at a

table, and the two stone steps leading up to the front door are a great place for kittens to play. Through the partially open gate we see a pathway to the woods, a portent of things to come. The curving lines, together with the soft, pleasing light, define the scene overall as home, happy, and safe. Nothing could possibly go wrong on such a beautiful day. The scene and mood are both set for the story to begin, and the open gate is waiting.

The title page, on the other hand, is a tour de force of graphic design. The decoration and the lovely hand lettering here add to the feeling of the setting, and also echo the traditional design and patterning of folk-art painting that Hyman studied as a student.

Hyman's medium of choice, a combination of pencil and acrylic paint on a Strathmore Crescent board, was perfect for Hyman's fast-working style of painting, because acrylic paint dries quickly and, if the picture called for it, she could combine other media with it almost at once.

Hyman didn't use models. Instead, she drew from her imagination and memory, and her art is often peopled with friends and family. She says she would read the story and literally see the pictures in her mind. They would slowly assemble themselves to journey down her arm to her hand and finally, through the pencil onto the boards.

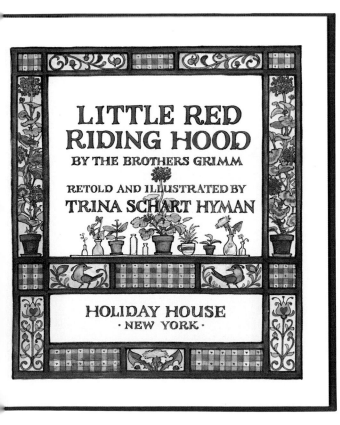

"I do a lot of thinking about how I want the book to look in every way. I design it in my head—I put it together like a movie while I'm walking in the morning, or sometimes in the middle of the night when I wake up and can't sleep. Then I put together a plain white paper dummy and cut up the galleys and begin to move the type around until I get it right.

"My favorite part of doing a book is when I've gotten all the drawings done and I can start the color—it's the color! I love color now, but I used to be very scared of it. And my very favorite part

pring green in
g. The wings
sides, and it
down. Jeremy
l dragon and
At that very
the once more,
fall. Thomas
d it with him
sh, all that he
ater.

is when I'm on the downhill slide, with like a couple of spreads to go and it's *WHOOO WHOOOOOOOOOOOOOOOOOO!*"

For all her love of color, Hyman has always been the consummate draftsman. No matter which book you look at, you will find the powerful skeleton of the drawings beneath all the color and drama. She was also a skilled printmaker, and a great deal of her power in black-and-white came from her ability to feel the emerging form as her line carved out its positive image from the negative white space behind it, creating just the right balance of form and white space.

"I love to work in black-and-white. Basically I'm a draftsman and a printmaker, and printmakers think in black-and-white."

*Magic in the Mist*, written by Margaret Mary Kimmel and published in 1975, was the perfect vehicle for this particular discipline. Set in Wales, this book is about a young boy named Thomas who lives at the edge of Borth bog and is studying to become a wizard. In the picture shown opposite, Thomas has just found a young dragon and is taking him home.

Drawn with a croquil pen and black ink, the expressive drawing shows Thomas striding purposefully into the wind. His hair is blown backward, and both cape and scarf are flying behind him. The curvilinear lines depict the impact of the wind, and because of those few well-placed lines we can almost feel the force of that wind as it blows across the rocky terrain. Held carefully in Thomas' left hand is Jeremy, his pet toad, and cradled gently in the crook of his arm is the baby dragon. The way Hyman has drawn the left foot in a clutching gesture shows us just how scared this little creature is.

The power and importance of black-and-white art has never really been fully appreciated in books for children, but so often this is the discipline that truly shows the strengths and abilities of the illustrator. When it is done well, it more than "illustrates" the story, as this work demonstrates.

Pen and ink is a particularly challenging medium, and when called upon to create areas of contrast and shading, cross-hatching is the most effective way to achieve that. By laying down continuous vertical lines side by side and then going over them with the same technique horizontally, one can achieve dark or black areas. The closer the lines, the darker the end result. Looking at this drawing, we can see how the black line used in many different patterns truly animates the characters and creates the swirling, blowing feeling of the wind. Deft cross-hatching with pen and ink depicts the weighty areas of the body and legs, and the swirling dots indicate the threat of moisture at any minute. The focus of the composition is the overall triangle that encompasses the figure itself and moves forward on an angle of motion. This simple but extremely effective layout carries a clear message of a boy on a mission.

It would be yet another grand fairy tale that would win a Caldecott Gold Medal for Trina Schart Hyman in 1985: *Saint George and the Dragon*, retold by Margaret Hodges.

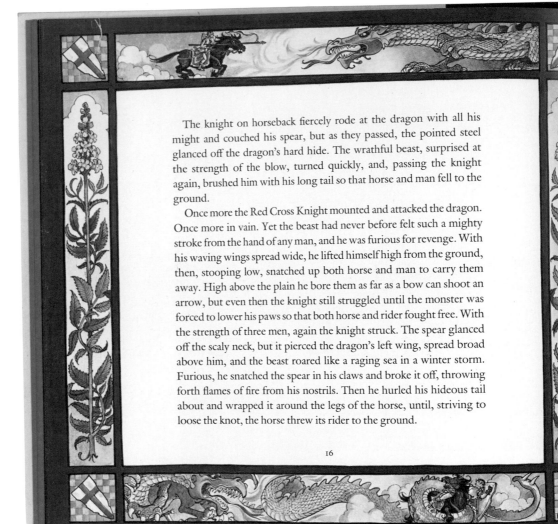

The knight on horseback fiercely rode at the dragon with all his might and couched his spear, but as they passed, the pointed steel glanced off the dragon's hard hide. The wrathful beast, surprised at the strength of the blow, turned quickly, and, passing the knight again, brushed him with his long tail so that horse and man fell to the ground.

Once more the Red Cross Knight mounted and attacked the dragon. Once more in vain. Yet the beast had never before felt such a mighty stroke from the hand of any man, and he was furious for revenge. With his waving wings spread wide, he lifted himself high from the ground, then, stooping low, snatched up both horse and man to carry them away. High above the plain he bore them as far as a bow can shoot an arrow, but even then the knight still struggled until the monster was forced to lower his paws so that both horse and rider fought free. With the strength of three men, again the knight struck. The spear glanced off the scaly neck, but it pierced the dragon's left wing, spread broad above him, and the beast roared like a raging sea in a winter storm. Furious, he snatched the spear in his claws and broke it off, throwing forth flames of fire from his nostrils. Then he hurled his hideous tail about and wrapped it around the legs of the horse, until, striving to loose the knot, the horse threw its rider to the ground.

16

The elegantly designed double-page spread shown here is classic Trina Schart Hyman, especially in the way the borders are used to continue the story. The manuscript was quite long, and so this design approach offered Hyman the opportunity to add to the pictorial content. On the left-hand page, the top border portrays the gallant knight charging the dragon. Along the bottom we see the continuing struggle. In each corner of the page is the shield of St. George, while the vertical borders depict the wildflower agrimony. Anglo-Saxons considered this plant vital in healing wounds after battle and in protecting against evil. In the white space created by the borders, we find the text; opposite is a large image of the main event.

In terms of show-and-tell, Hyman's career is unique in several ways, but one aspect in particular stands out. She first began illustrating for children in 1961, and during those

early years she did a huge amount of textbook illustration featuring children and the everyday world in which they live. This meant accurately chronicling the lifestyles of those periods. During this time, the world went from the paper datebook to the electronic PDA, and from radio to television and computers.

When asked about this, she replied, "Somebody ought to give me a lifetime achievement award just for the size of the body of work!"

Well, on November 3, 2005, someone did. At the opening night of the twenty-fifth anniversary of the Original Art Exhibition at the Society of Illustrators in New York, Trina Schart Hyman was awarded the Society's first posthumous Lifetime Achievement Award. It's remarkable to see what a grand artist grew out of the shy Little Red.

*Changing Woman and Her Sisters*, published in 2006, was Hyman's last book.

# BRYAN COLLIER
## Angels in the Snow

"It wasn't the story. I don't remember reading it—I just followed the images and the boy looked like me. . . . It smacked of my whole life and what we did in the neighborhood. And it had this 'voice' and I didn't even read the story, but it spoke to you. *It was like the friend you never knew you had, and the friend looked like you.*"

Born on January 31, 1967, in Salisbury, Maryland, Collier was the youngest of six children whose mother worked for a Head Start program. Sometimes she would bring home games or books for her children. One of the books she brought home and gave to the young Collier was *The Snowy Day* by Ezra Jack Keats. Who could have imagined that many years later Collier would be sitting on the stage at the 2001 Coretta Scott King Award Breakfast as winner of the first Ezra Jack Keats New Illustrator Award, for *Uptown*, which Collier both wrote and illustrated?

Although he was born in Salisbury, Collier grew up in Pocomoke, Maryland, and had a very stable childhood surrounded by family and friends. Whenever his mother brought new books home, he was the first to jump on them. Along with *The Snowy Day*, his other favorite book was *Harold and the Purple Crayon*, by Crockett Johnson. For a young black child born the year before Dr. Martin Luther King, Jr. was assassinated, that purple crayon must have seemed like a passport to all kinds of possibilities. In those days in the South, people didn't move around as much as they do now.

When he was five years old, Collier moved next door into his grandmother's house because his grandmother was alone, and that worked just fine for Collier. His grandmother was very active, and spent a lot of time at the senior center doing ceramics and making quilts. She also loved to make landscapes from bits of fabric. At the time, it didn't really make an impression on him. But then one day, when he was fifteen, he wandered into the art room at school and started to paint. It was a turning point in his life.

"I just started to paint that day and that thing picked me. It was like, 'I choose you and this is what you are going to do.' I mean, you can't escape something like that. And it's been that strong every single day, whether I paint or not."

It is exactly that kind of passion and commitment that is apparent in all of Collier's work, and that comes across to the viewer. Each picture seems to challenge itself to be as good, if not better, than the one that came before.

In 1985, Collier won first place in a congressional competition in Washington, D.C., and later that year, was awarded a scholarship to the Pratt Institute in New York City through their national talent search competition.

The high energy of the city perfectly suited this adventurous young man from the South; he loved every minute of it. Pratt and Brooklyn were the right places at the right time. There was an influx of young musicians and artists moving into Brooklyn, and people like Spike Lee were a real presence on the art scene. Everything seemed to be coming together for Collier. He discovered film and loved music and soon found himself very much at home.

Pratt was an exciting place for Collier, but he was never completely enraptured with any particular artist or technique. He did discover Caravaggio, a sixteenth-century Italian master of Baroque painting, and was completely in awe of his magical ability to handle dark and light, creating intense drama. But mostly Collier was focused on fine-tuning his own art form.

One day when he was first living in New York City, as he was riding an uptown train for Lincoln Center, he missed his stop and got out in Harlem. This turned out to be a life-changing experience, which he still recounts with awe:

"Oh, man, when I came to Harlem for the first time it was like I was here before. I was trying to get to the Met, and I was lost. I took the A train all the way up, and I got out at this stop and something connected with the sidewalk—I just knew I had been here before. So then I walked all the way downtown through the streets of Harlem to the Met. But I knew the place, and I have always been fascinated with Harlem from that day on. There's just something about Harlem."

He started working with the Harlem Hospital Center Art Studio, eventually becoming the art director of a program called Unity Through Murals. This program was designed to bring self-taught artists into the Harlem community. While working in this program, Collier discovered his love for kids and gained a great respect for their innate intelligence.

"I love working with kids—they get it, you know. I was with a class of five-year-olds recently talking about doing books, and I asked them a question: 'What do you need to do or have to make a children's book?' 'You need a purpose,' was their answer."

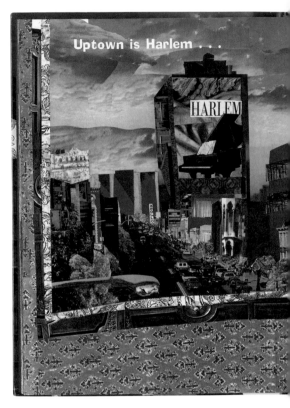

Collier's first foray into publishing began with an appointment with Laura Godwin, then associate publisher for Henry Holt's Books for Young Readers division. Godwin found the soft-spoken and earnest young man interesting and loved his work, and she began to talk with him about ideas. His excitement about Harlem and the painting studio and its mural project became the catalyst.

"I took my portfolio as an illustrator to Laura Godwin, and before I knew it she wanted me to write, too. I didn't know anything about size or proportion of book design, and she just told me to relax and tell her what I did know about Harlem and the studio and what was so special. Things like that. And I could do that. So I talked about the murals and how painting them really let me see Harlem. I went everywhere on foot because I walked around with my painting cart all through the streets. I pulled out all the images I knew about—like uptown is a row of brownstones that look like chocolate . . . or chicken and waffles . . . and gradually I became comfortable with these images and they worked. So I went to work and I guess I had done about eight big images and then found out I'd have to do them over in book format. It was a long, drawn-out, arduous process, but Laura Godwin held my hand every step of the way.

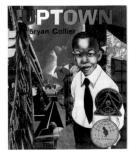

"It took me five years, but it taught me how to make a book from beginning to end, and it turned out the way I wanted." That book was *Uptown*.

In the double page spread shown here, the artist has literally presented a view of Harlem to us. Well balanced in composition and anchored by the strong vertical of the young boy himself, the scene is both mysterious and inviting. Created entirely in watercolor and torn paper collage, the picture is three-dimensional and full of richly subdued color—except for the sky, with its glowing pink sunset. The word *Harlem* on

the central building just above the image of a piano suggests music, jazz, and dancing, and just up the street we see the sign for the Apollo Theater. It's early evening, and the buildings are lit, adding a warmth and intimacy to the moment. The young boy seems very much at home and pleased to share his neighborhood with us as he looks right out at us to see if we like it, too.

Collier achieves both a feeling of intimacy and the call of the street outside by using the gray and burgundy patterned wallpaper as a demarcation zone defining the walls of the room. But the most important thing is the art's ability to "tell a story," to create a sense of place.

Unlike most illustrators, there is no sketch or dummy stage in the making of Collier's books. He needs to work directly on the final surface to be in touch with the feel of the work as it progresses. Any changes will be made directly onto that finished surface board or paper. When working on a landscape or a cityscape of brownstones, Collier might begin with a photo of the intended background and then work over that with paint and collage, going back and forth until it feels and looks right. When patterns and textures are specific, he will look for wallpaper or blue jeans or a sunset, and cut pieces out of a magazine. He is always on the lookout for collage material that has subject matter close to the needs of the book he is working on, or material that might perhaps relate to a future project. He then proceeds with the initial image in watercolor, laying pieces of collage down and building the picture and composition at the same time.

Though *Uptown* seemed dificult at first, powerful imagery soon took over and pro-pelled the story line. Collier knew exactly what he needed to "show and tell." And he didn't have to translate someone else's voice. His images fell into place from all those days of painting the streets of Harlem from his cart. However, his next book—*Freedom River*, written by Doreen Rappaport—was a different kind of challenge.

Maureen Sullivan at Hyperion's Jump at the Sun imprint was his editor on *Freedom River* and, again, a guiding force at the beginning of his career. This book was a big challenge since it had a noble theme, a great deal of excitement, and most challenging of all, it all takes place entirely at night. The story features John Parker, a freed slave who

decides to help other slaves escape to freedom. He does this by rowing them across the Ohio River at night from the Kentucky shore and then handing them over to a safe house.

"*Freedom River* was an extraordinary journey for me because I finally had to step away from the text to find the key to creating the pictures. I knew the river was important, and the bravery of it all, and it took place at night. And then I felt the rhythm of the book—it had the commands ROW ROW and RUN RUN—and finally I put myself into the story and walked through it."

Collier realized the river was the most important element. The river was freedom, and everything depended on it. Its restless surface was in constant motion. From the endpapers to the faces of the people in the vignettes, you will see curving striations that capture the feeling of the ever-moving waters of the river.

In the picture shown opposite, we see John Parker rowing steadily and forcefully back to the Ohio shore. It is evening, with a sliver of a moon in a dark blue sky. The clouds are dark in color and ominous in nature. Small hints of red suggest the end of sunset, and as John's right paddle breaks the water's surface it disturbs the moon's reflection. His broad back and shoulders reflect his strength of purpose, and his clothing perfectly matches the nighttime world around him. But the jagged edges of the head-lands and river suggest danger. As he pulls strongly upriver, he gazes anxiously at lights in a few windows close by, wondering if the people inside can see him, too. By not making it a totally black night, we are able to see the suggestion of a beach on the shore and the low hills in the distance. And although he is large in form, John appears vulnerable as he watches for any sign of chase. The powerful underlying composition, together with the collage technique, gives this picture a truly three-dimensional feeling. The viewer feels just outside the triangle of action as John is almost upon them. On the facing text page page in the book, a vignette of a young girl (shown here) carries the linear striations of the moving river across her face and shoulders. This simple design element tells us that the river is always moving through everyone's lives, never stopping.

The book that made the biggest impact on Bryan Collier personally and that in many ways was his biggest challenge was *Martin's Big Words: The Life of Dr. Martin Luther King, Jr.*, again written by Doreen Rappaport. The subject matter alone was overwhelming at first. How does an artist go about depicting an almost mythical figure while at the same time conveying his humanity?

"In illustrating the life of Dr. King, I needed a vehicle to drive it all the way to the end. Something to tie it all together. I wanted to do something different because so much has already been done."

Ultimately Collier decided that the stained-glass windows of his neighborhood church, Emmanuel Baptist, were the answer. He saw the coming together of all the colors in the glass as a metaphor for the coming together of all the races—almost as though one could see the dream in the glass and then look through it and see its reality in the world outside.

The double-page spread shown here portrays Martin as a young boy stopping to drink from a water fountain outside a store. His mother stands beside him and holds his left hand in hers. In her left hand she carries a book, perhaps a Bible. It's Sunday, and they are on their way to church.

The large plate-glass window of the storefront reflects a multitude of images from the street, but most noticeable is the outstretched hand of Martin as he points to a WHITE ONLY sign printed on the fountain next to his. To the left of the building is a narrow alley, and hanging there is an American flag. Behind it is a blue sky with puffy clouds and what could be the wooden tower of the church in the background.

The underlying rectangular composition both presents and anchors this compelling

moment, as the sidewalk becomes the stage and the large glass window allows the viewer to go back into the deep space behind it. The two fountains and the sign also act as a separation between the street and the inside of the store, suggesting that perhaps it, too, is "white only." The structures in the alley look old, and the white paint on the wooden window frame is crumbling to reveal areas of bare wood. The suggestion here is that this is the poor side of town, although Martin and his mother are dressed in their Sunday best and are indeed "as good as anyone."

The window also reflects the buildings across the street and suggests the small windows facing the back of the building. The overall feeling is one of confusion and objects crowded one upon another. It's unsettling. Nothing seems to make sense—in just the same way as the racist sign makes no sense.

The black-and-white pattern of the mother's dress and the casual drape of her shoulder bag bring her forward in the picture plane, giving her strength and presence. And the black pants and white shirt of Martin feature him as the central figure here as he points to the offending sign. By keeping the color limited and subdued, the feeling of the moment

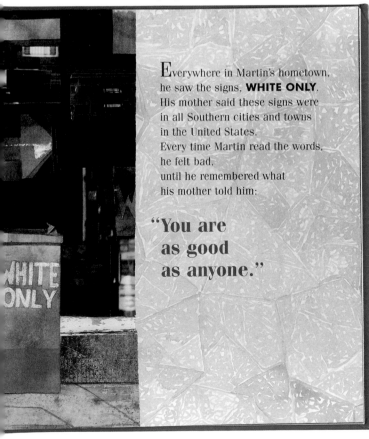

Everywhere in Martin's hometown, he saw the signs, **WHITE ONLY**. His mother said these signs were in all Southern cities and towns in the United States. Every time Martin read the words, he felt bad, until he remembered what his mother told him:

"You are as good as anyone."

is portrayed as one of thoughtfulness and caution. The use of bright colors or lighter areas would immediately change the somber feeling of this moment.

The right-hand edge of the picture sits on a gray mottled surface. On closer inspection, we recognize this surface as the stained-glass windows of the church. Readers are artfully directed to look through this glass to see what follows as we turn the page.

*Martin's Big Words* received the 2002 Coretta Scott King Honor Award for illustration and a Caldecott Honor.

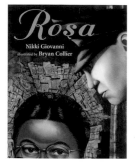

For Bryan Collier's book *Rosa*—written in elegant prose by Nikki Giovanni, an award-winning poet, writer, and activist—collage was once again the perfect medium.

In August 2004 Collier visited the towns of Montgomery and Selma in Alabama. When he arrived, the first impression he had was of intense heat, and he would remember that as he determined his palette for the book. In his note at the beginning of the book he says: "I wanted the reader to feel in that heat a foreshadowing, an uneasy quiet before the storm." And his choice of color for this story truly reflects that feeling. The use of yellow with the dark-hued tones of the other colors perfectly captures the heat and the overall quiet fear being portrayed.

In the page shown opposite, the small group of people waiting for the bus—as they have done so many times before—looks tired. They most certainly have no sense of the monumental event that is about to take place. The strong figure of Rosa Parks stands in line, a calm expression on her face. The triangular composition of her form is anchored powerfully to center stage. Behind her, the long bus has pulled up to the curb. The color of Rosa's clothing, in understated hues of brown with different textured surfaces, is in perfect harmony against the hot yellow-green of the bus. In the background we see a white capitol building with flags flying, symbolic perhaps of the historic moment to come. The sky above is laden with storm clouds waiting to be unleashed.

By treating this moment the way he has, Collier has set the tone for what happens as Rosa Parks decides not to give up her seat. It was not some grand scheme planned ahead of time. She was just suddenly tired, very tired of the many things she had to do in her life because she happened to be black. That's precisely what makes her a truly heroic figure. A hardworking middle-class woman, she symbolized her whole race with quiet dignity and power. All of that comes across in this remarkable illustration.

*Rosa* was awarded the 2006 Coretta Scott King Award and a Caldecott Honor. Looking at all of these books together, the overall feeling is that none could have been illustrated in any other medium, so perfectly does the slightly different use and application of the collage technique fit each. Collage provides the texture and tactile quality needed to convey the emotion of the story, and, together with watercolor, creates a perfect harmony of light and color. Texture here is used visually, the way strong adjectives might emphasize an emotion or a moment in time.

"Collage is more than just an art style. Collage is all about bringing different elements together. Once you form a sensibility about connection, how different elements relate to each other, you deepen your understanding of yourself and others."

Bryan Collier has indeed perfected his voice and found his own unique purpose—just the way all of those five-year-olds knew he would.

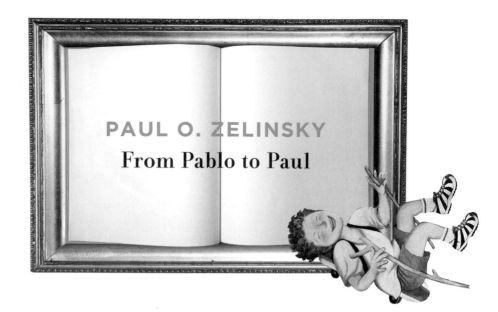

# PAUL O. ZELINSKY
## From Pablo to Paul

"My parents were members of the Art Institute of Chicago and they would take me with them whenever they went. As a kid I enjoyed these trips and the scale and drama of the building, and there were so many pictures. I had no use for the classical art, but as for the modern wing—the Matisses, the Calders, the Picassos—I loved it!"

I wonder how many people would think of Paul Zelinsky and Pablo Picasso as having anything at all in common. And yet on further inspection they share many similarities. Early in Picasso's career, he painted realistically before beginning his exploration of myriad styles. And all through his extraordinary career, he expressed himself not only on paper and canvas, but also in mixed-media and sculpture. Whatever his style of expression, however, his work was always classic in its interpretation. His line was either energetic and powerful or gently curvilinear and sensuous. His color was often bold and clear or sometimes more monochromatic and intellectual in feeling. He had a passion for his work, loved experimenting with scale and design, and of course had a great sense of humor. He taught us all how to look at things with a fresh eye.

Zelinsky's work also demonstrates great shifts in style, technique, and expression. Beginning with black-and-white drawings for *How I Hunted the Little Fellows*, a work both realistic and classic in nature, he then shifted to the world of Italian Renaissance, painting *Hansel and Gretel*, only to be followed by a rollicking zany style for *The Wheels on the Bus*, a total departure from the "classic" Zelinsky we thought we knew so well. And *Swamp Angel*, a masterful accomplishment painted in the folk-art style, showed an extraordinary use of scale and color throughout. So perhaps the stretch from Pablo to Paul is not so hard to contemplate, after all.

Paul Zelinsky was born in Evanston, Illinois, in 1953, but grew up in nearby Wilmette and went to the public schools there. His father was a math professor at Northwestern University, and his mother was a medical illustrator. When Zelinsky was not quite three years old, his father received a Fullbright Fellowship, and the family moved to Kyoto, Japan, for a year. Upon returning to Wilmette, the Zelinsky household never looked quite the same. The year in Kyoto had heavily influenced their taste. Their new home was filled with furniture and decorations from Japan. Japanese prints and paintings hung on the walls. The family wore kimonos for bathrobes, and they were constantly visited by friends they had met abroad.

For a young boy who already loved making pictures, it was a fun house to grow up in. There were lots of art supplies around, and his mother was often working on drawings or an occasional oil painting. She encouraged her young son to draw, too. Zelinsky simply can't remember a time when he didn't love drawing.

"Long before I went to preschool I loved making pictures, and even though we all made pictures in school, I liked making my pictures at home the best. My mother would be working and I would, too."

As a child, Zelinsky's mother read to him often. He enjoyed reading the Little Golden Books. Margaret Wise Brown's books were among his favorites early on, and (a little) later he loved the work of William Pene de Bois. However, the classic illustrations by John Tenniel in *Alice in Wonderland* were special to Zelinsky. The mystery, fantasy, and magical use of scale all stirred his imagination and left their marks on his mind's eye.

As an adolescent, Zelinsky became a huge science-fiction fan and scoured the shelves of the village library for anything remotely connected to this genre. As he considered a future career, he thought he might become an architect or an artist, but he wasn't really sure. His high school art teacher told him that Yale College's art program was as fine as its academics. He applied and was accepted. It was a good choice.

Zelinsky really enjoyed Yale. Apart from art classes he also took a few science courses and dabbled in many subjects, which he found very satisfying. And then one day the college offered a special course on the picture book with a teacher by the name of Maurice Sendak. It was the first class Sendak ever taught. The course was called The History of the Picture Book, and in it he introduced the work of seminal children's book illustrators of

Victorian England, from Kate Greenaway to Randolph Caldecott all the way to Edward Ardizzone. Great emphasis was placed on the attitudes toward children in Victorian times and how such attitudes affected the making of picture books. The second part of the class dealt with the making of a book. The opportunity to hear Sendak talk about the history of children's books was a gift for Zelinsky. Always the consummate communicator, Sendak lit a fire in the classroom. "Sendak's class gave me and everyone else an enlarged understanding about what children's books could be and what they meant to him. He was incredibly effective in communicating, and my immediate feeling was— I could do this!

"One of the most important things that jumped out at me during this class was the idea of rhythm in picture books. . . . It opened up a whole new way of looking [at books]."

There were also discussions about the power of black-and-white art, and the work of Albrecht Dürer, and the class took a good look at woodblock printing.

The appreciation Zelinsky gained for his illustration forebears led to admiration of many of his own peers, as diverse a group as Marc Simont and the illustrations he made for *The Philharmonic Gets Dressed* and Margot Zemach. About her, he says, "I always felt no matter what she did, it had this formal strength to it, she was incredible."

After graduating with a B.A. from Yale, Zelinsky went to the Tyler School of Art in Philadelphia and completed an M.F.A. in painting. Fortunately for him, his first year was spent studying in Rome, where he had access to all its extraordinary museums and architectural splendor. It was the beginning of a love affair with that great city.

Following his graduation from Tyler, and a brief stint as an art teacher, he put together a portfolio of work and went to New York. His first book, written by Avi and titled *Emily Upham's Revenge*, was published in 1978. It was illustrated in black-and-white, and when it came out, Donna Brooks, an editor at Dodd Mead, saw it and immediately remembered

Zelinsky's portfolio. She was looking for an illustrator for a manuscript called *How I Hunted the Little Fellows*, by Russian author Boris Zhitkov. Zelinsky was commissioned to illustrate it.

The black-and-white jacket shown here is beautifully designed, with the title box serving a definite purpose. The front of the jacket is compelling, with the partially covered face of the young boy half in shadow. The degree of density from black to white not only creates a three-dimensional effect but also a sense of mystery. The composition shows the boy half in hiding, as if he knows that what he is about to do is wrong. The title box and hull of the ship help conceal him. The technique here is quite extraordinary—as the cross-hatching ranges from almost solid black to very fine lines on the boy's face and short hair. By keeping the top half of the hull white without outlines, the image takes on an eerie, ghostly feeling. It is an uneasy image. We don't know the story yet, but somehow we feel that something bad is going to happen. This picture really tells the story right away.

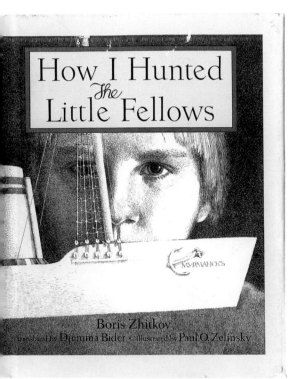

The back of the jacket shows the stern of the little ship and a shaft of white light coming in through the window behind it. It's here that we can see the painstaking application of the pen in the shadows on the window frame and then, more boldly, in the weight of the long curtain. One half is in shadow and the other half in light. Both the window wall and the wall behind the ship seem to act as a stage presenting the story to us and urging us to open the book.

This story was a perfect match for this imaginative young artist at the beginning of his career. It was also a great vehicle to present his sensitive handling of a difficult medium and to showcase his ability to create a sense of time, place, and character.

Zelinsky must feel passionate about a story before he will agree to illustrate it. His goal is to constantly seek out the perfect visual voice to tell each story. A good example of this is the work he did for *Swamp Angel*, written by Anne Isaacs and published in 1994. *Swamp Angel* presented many different kinds of challenges, not the least of which was scale. But as soon as he read the manuscript, he couldn't wait to do the book.

Understanding a little more about Zelinsky's training explains his ability as a painter. Nothing really scares him. His great technical skill enables him to experiment with a wide range of styles and media. *Swamp Angel*, for example, required a great deal of research on the technique of the folk-art painters of the nineteenth century.

In a book from the National Gallery collection, he found a painting by Linton Park called *Flax Scutching Bee*. Because of the scarcity of art supplies in rural Pennsylvania circa 1900, it had been painted on bed ticking. This scrounging for materials reminded Zelinsky of some wonderful paper he had long admired—a paper-thin cherry wood veneer. It seemed an apt choice. Here was a story about a primitive woodswoman, so of course it should be painted on wood! And it should be done in the style of folk-art painting.

"Clearly the medium would be oil paint, and as I studied these folk-art paintings, I discovered I needed to finish the backgrounds first, as much as possible, let them dry, and then paint objects on top. This separated foreground from background in a blocky kind of way; it's what I saw in folk painting. And then I looked very carefully at how they painted people, because there really did seem to be a formula there, which I hope I came close to finding."

The double-page spread seen here is an example of folk art at its best. In true folk-art tradition, it shows the fine detail of the scene. On the left-hand page, we see Swamp Angel and Thundering Tarnation locked in deadly combat as they wrestle their way

Locked in a bear hug, Swamp Angel and Thundering Tarnation wrestled across the hills of Tennessee. They stirred up so much dust that those hills are still called the Great Smoky Mountains. They fought three days and three nights without a break.

On the fourth day, they wrestled their way into a lake fifty feet deep. Tarnation pinned Angel to the muddy bottom with one of his gigantic paws.

across the Tennessee hills, stirring up mountains of dust. In the distance is a small piece of blue sky with a horizon line, and as we cross the gutter between the pages, the scene on the right-hand page reveals a crystal-blue lake. There are trees around the lake, a pair of coots swimming together, a noble blue heron posing on a small island (which, upon closer inspection, turns out to be a bear's bottom), and a man in a boat peacefully fishing, unaware that Swamp Angel is pinned to the lake floor by the massive bear. On the lake surface, all seems calm and peaceful, but the water is crystal clear, so we can see the drama taking place.

Zelinsky's spare but subtle use of color is a hallmark of his work here. The final pictures were painted in oils on cherry, maple, and birch veneer with a clear varnish

finish. The book was awarded a Caldecott Honor in 1995.

In the making of any book, each artist has his or her own way of doing things. In Zelinsky's case, he takes the following steps: His process begins with the reading of the manuscript to decide if the story is absolutely right for him. Then he breaks the story down page by page, marking the manuscript. The next stage is making thumbnail sketches of the sequential story line and action.

"At this point I may still not know exactly what I'm doing, but I will know if it is wrong. Then if it doesn't find its own way, I have to find a way to get into it. So then I'll go to my art books and browse until I find something that feels right."

When Zelinsky's great-grandmother was seventy years old, she was given a set of oil paints. It turned out she was a natural painter. Soon she had produced a scene from *Hansel and Gretel* as a birthday present for Paul's older sister. Paul grew up loving that painting. It was the wish to tap into the feelings his great-grandmother's picture had stirred in him when he was a young child that led him to propose his own version of *Hansel and Gretel*.

"I didn't want my paintings to look anything like my grandmother's painting. I just wanted the feeling and mood I remembered. It had to do with the light and that kind of evening, and the feeling of the woods around the witch's cottage. At first I thought that I would like my pictures to look something like a Dutch genre painting of perhaps Van Ostade, or then again maybe Breugel. Finally I decided to replicate a Renaissance style of painting and it felt right to me."

This is the essence of Zelinsky's work. The most important thing to him is finding a story that captivates. Then begins the search for the feeling and mood the pictures must convey, and finally, finding the style of painting that fits the story like a glove.

There's no doubt that his year studying in Rome studying was pivotal in his artistic career, and it comes as no surprise that Zelinsky chose the Italian Renaissance style of painting for *Hansel and Gretel* and, of course, for *Rapunzel*, the winner of the 1998 Caldecott Medal.

The Renaissance style was a perfect choice for *Rapunzel*, a tale, as it turned out, with some Italian roots; a tale full of twists and turns set in a rustic landscape. As always, Zelinsky creates a powerful sense of time and place—the result of painstaking research. With one glance at the spread shown opposite, we know this is the Italian countryside, with its walled town full of towers and arches and campaniles bathed in a gentle light. Flora and fauna surround us—notice a bee hard at work at the bottom of the left-hand page. And the overall color is that of the Tuscany farmlands. The blue sky above seems to cradle the stylized clouds as they gracefully float away.

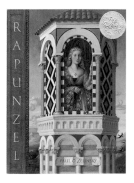

This picture shows the approaching happy ending. The family, now reunited, moves slowly toward the town. In front of them, the cat—still wary of the current turn of events—looks up at the prince with some concern. As is typical of Zelinsky, we see the touches that make the scene human and compelling. There are holes in the prince's shoes and dirt on the hem of Rapunzel's dress. The babies are both held with great tenderness. And there is no doubting the look of wonderment and affection in the eyes of Rapunzel as she gazes at her prince. As they move, the breeze catches their garments, so we glimpse the intricate designs and colors of the fabrics. Coming up the slope in front of them, a farmer and his

small child get ready to greet the family. Meanwhile, the blue river snakes around the valley and under the bridge. The distant hills appear to encircle and protect the scene. Once again, we recognize the hallmark of any Zelinsky book: this picture is a moment captured in time. It feels wonderful—there is a great sense of peacefulness and hope. The mood and feeling have been established, and all is right with the picture and the story.

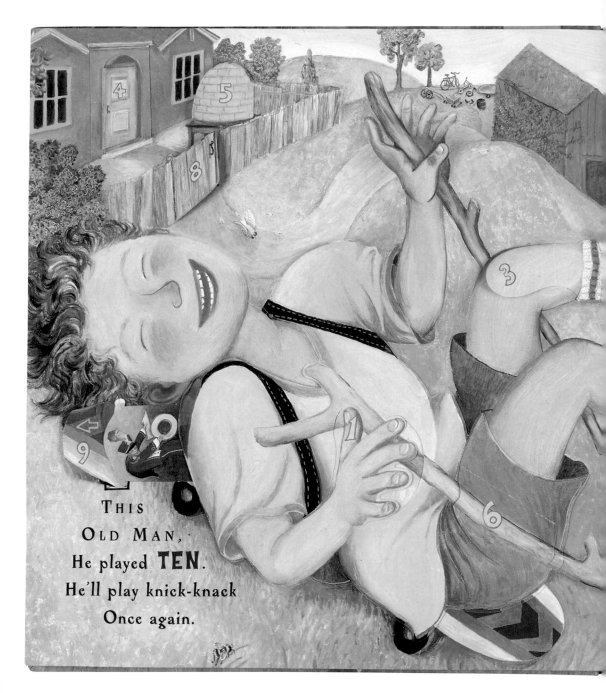

In *Knick-Knack Paddywhack!*, published in 2002, we see yet another facet of Zelinsky's repertoire. When he figured out that "This Old Man" could become a mechanical book like *The Wheels On the Bus*, he researched the song and began plotting—sound, rhythm, words, and action. Soon he realized he was hearing the rhythm of a book, just as he'd been taught to do by Maurice Sendak in the class that had lit such a spark in him.

With a KNICK-KNACK
PADDYWHACK!
Give the dog a bone.
These old men
came
rolling...

Every page in the book has tabs, pop-ups, and sliding levers—action actually happens. Movable parts reveal hidden pictures, and on this next-to-last spread the final arrow tab, when pulled, causes twelve little men and dogs to roll down the hill together.

On the final spread of *Knick-Knack Paddywhack!*, we see all of the characters performing in an orchestra. The book is Zelinsky's Broadway musical. What will he do next?

# DAVID WIESNER
## What If?

First and foremost, David Wiesner is a storyteller, a "what if?" kind of person. He has an insatiable curiosity about life, and a wonderful sense of humor. He ponders the improbable with quiet pleasure and then creates the impossible with great glee. The starting place is always the same: *In the beginning was the concept*—one strong enough to get the senses reeling with anticipation.

"When I was nine years old my teacher read a Ray Bradbury story called 'All in a Summer Day' to us in class. The story was about how kids treat each other and how incredibly cruel they can be at times. I can't believe she read it to us. But for me the science-fiction aspect of it all taking place on Venus completely impacted me and sucked me in. It was then that I found my ability to create a world visually as it was going along. . . . I can remember to this day the feeling of it."

Born in Bridgewater, New Jersey, in 1956, Wiesner grew up in a neighborhood surrounded by woods and undeveloped land. There were kids of all ages to play with in a time when kids ran free in their neighborhoods.

"There was something going on every day just out the back door. The whole world was waiting out there, and my friends and I played all over the neighborhood, sometimes down along the brook making complicated dams, sometimes sneaking off into the woods behind enemy lines, and we each had a collection of great sticks. There was nothing better than finding a really great stick that could be used for all kinds of make-believe things. I watched enough TV to soak up the popular culture and cartoons, but it was all the old stuff I liked best. The black-and-white movies of the Marx Brothers and those fifties scary monster movies were my favorites."

The youngest of five siblings, Wiesner's childhood was a very busy and happy time. He began to draw almost as soon as he could hold a crayon. There was no regular bedtime reading, although occasionally his mother would read him a scary story or two.

By the time he was five years old, Wiesner was painting pictures at an easel in kindergarten. Soon after that he began drawing dinosaurs that he'd seen in books. His friends all knew he liked to draw, but mostly it was a private thing. Then one day he was watching cartoons on television, and an artist called John Nagy appeared on screen, and he began talking about learning to paint. Wiesner was hooked.

Childhood books for Wiesner consisted mostly of nonfiction. He loved the World Book Encyclopedias and the *History of the Earth*, also published by World Book—in particular, the section on dinosaurs with the drawings by Charles Knight. Also included in his reading were the Time-Life series of books. In junior high school he read a lot of comic books, and both copied them and drew his own versions. He had grasped the storytelling power of this genre and was fascinated by its sequential aspect.

In the stacks at the local library he came across books of artists and found their paintings spellbinding. He discovered Bruegel's *Landscape with the Fall of Icarus* and could hardly believe his eyes. He vividly recalls its impact:

"This painting was incredible. There were vast amounts of story happening here. There were all these little people doing so many different things. They were plowing the fields and carrying things and taking a cart to market, and then right over in the corner is Icarus plunging into the water, barely noticed!"

He also discovered Albrecht Dürer, Leonardo da Vinci, and Michelangelo, and marveled at their richly detailed work. By the age of ten he had discovered the Surrealists and made an immediate connection with some of the "weird stuff" he had seen in monster movies. One piece stands out in his memory:

"On a trip to the Philadelphia Museum of Fine Art I saw *The Large Glass* by Marcel Duchamp—it was amazing. I mean I had no idea what it was about, but even the story behind it was great. Apparently, in shipping, the crate was dropped and the glass had this huge crack in it and Duchamp said, 'Keep it. I love it!'"

Salvador Dali, another Surrealist artist, was also a wonderful discovery and his *Persistence of Memory* made an especially huge impression on Wiesner when he came across it at the Museum of Modern Art in New York. It was a small painting—but it was huge in suggestion. At the time, seeing this painting was a clear signal to this young art student that painting and story, no matter how unusual, could coexist.

The artists of the Dada and Surrealist movements had all been young and had experienced the horrors of the first World War, and their work was a reaction to man and machine and the waste of young lives. Wiesner continued his interest in these painters through high school. Discovering artists who went through an intelligent thought process before creating things was a major event for Wiesner. It directed his thinking into new channels of possibility. In the beginning was the concept. Eventually all of this would come together in his own role as a visual storyteller of extraordinary events.

However, from the ages of twelve to fourteen, he was still very dedicated to comic books. *Peanuts* was a favorite, and he loved *MAD* magazine, but Marvel Comics were his passion, especially *Nick Fury, Agent of S.H.I.E.L.D.*, first drawn by Jack Kirby. Wiesner's strong connection with comic books would prove pivotal in his thinking as a children's book illustrator. The double-page format offers ample white space that can be broken up and used to tell a story with few or no words. And utilizing the panel format was a great tool to either extend or compress the timeline of a story. A lot of little panels could act in the same way that a slow-motion camera works. A longer horizontal panel could define and isolate a moment.

Wiesner also loved going to the movies. In his senior year in high school he studied filmmaking and actually made a couple of black-and-white movies. A lot of his visual thinking still incorporates unusual "camera" angles and well-defined moments of drama. Just as a movie moves constantly forward, so indeed do his books.

Wiesner's decision to go to art school came when he was almost fifteen. An alumni from his high school who was then attending the Rhode Island School of Design (RISD) gave a presentation about the kind of work and projects he was involved with at the school. Wiesner knew immediately that this was the school for him.

The first three years at RISD were fairly general in focus. Then Wiesner decided to take a course in children's books. The teacher was David Macaulay, a talented children's book author and illustrator whose books *Cathedral* and *Pyramid* had already been enormously successful. Macaulay's class focused on the use of pen and ink and was geared specifically to the making of books. This was when Wiesner began to feel that books were where his work might fit in.

Another class introduced Wiesner to the work of Arthur Rackham and Edmund Dulac. He could hardly believe his eyes. Here were beautiful paintings, combined with great narrative power. Soon he came across the work of illustrators Trina Schart Hyman and Leo and Diane Dillon. He knew the Dillons' work from their science-fiction illustration. It was inspiring to see that they also made picture books. Here was yet another sign that he was on the right path.

"Storytelling was the big part of what I liked to do with the art I was making, rather than being a painter and painting paintings. It was the storytelling process that motivated the pictures. In fact, now that I think about it, there was always a narrative quality to the pictures I was making."

The final step into children's books came when Trina Schart Hyman, then the art director of *Cricket* magazine, came to RISD in 1978. She saw Wiesner's work and offered him an assignment to do a full-color cover for a 1979 issue. The painting he did was called *The Giant Cricket Expedition.*

All told, *Cricket* commissioned four full-color covers by Wiesner. One of them was *Air Raid*, which depicted a flying frog and was the genesis for Wiesner's book *Tuesday*, which won Wiesner his first Caldecott Medal, in 1992.

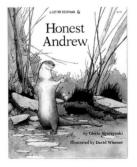

In May 1979 Wiesner went to New York, where I had just started an agency representing children's book illustrators. I had been the assistant art director for *Cricket* and, of course, already knew Wiesner's work. I had a feeling that this was a young genius just waiting for an opportunity, so, happily, I invited him to join Dilys Evans Fine Illustration.

The first editor to give Wiesner a book to illustrate was Barbara Lucas, then editorial director of Harcourt Brace Jovanovich's children's book department. That book, *Honest Andrew*, written by Gloria Skurzynski, was a two-color title. A picture from the book made it into the first Original Art Exhibition in 1980 at the Master Eagle Gallery in New York and subsequently appeared in the *New York Times*. David Wiesner was on his way.

It was Dorothy Briley, then at Lothrop, Lee and Shepard Books, however, who would turn out to be Wiesner's longtime editor and a good friend. She, too, recognized the extraordinary talent of this thoughtful young man, and she edited his very first full-color book, *Free Fall*, a wordless picture book that won a Caldecott Honor in 1989.

*Free Fall* was an extraordinary fantasy, following a young boy's dream adventure. The pictures are sequential and skillfully metamorphose one into the other as the pages turn from one to the next. The pencil dummy for the book was actually one long unfolding scroll of paper that the eye tracked rather like a movie.

This wordless dream journey is painted in watercolor with very little white space, and the color is applied in a series of thin washes. Ultramarine blue, Payne's gray, and raw umber intermingle to create a dreamlike atmosphere.

In the double-page spread shown above, the hero of the story is reclining, looking down at a gathering of elegantly dressed tiny people who are gazing at a map that is spread out before them. The scene is set inside a large, cavernous structure drawn in the style of Piranesi, the eighteenth-century Italian architect and engraver. As we approach the right-hand margin, the building begins changing back into the rock from which it was carved. Tall Ionic columns, rows of horizontal stone steps, and a flagstone floor all help establish the elegant nature of the space. Perched on the boy's right

shoulder are the story's three main protagonists. The largest figure, wrapped in a long gray coat and wearing a cap, seems to be gesticulating for attention. On the left-hand page, we see a closed book with a long piece of greenish tail protruding from within. A group of little figures sit on the book as if to keep what looks very much like a dragon from an earlier encounter safely inside. A feeling of deep space is created by the view down the hall below the bended leg of the reclining boy. This perspective increases the scale of this strange building. In the background, we see more steps leading to the outside and more rock formations. Finally, in the bottom right-hand, there are five pigs just looking around. The great use of scale here, something that Wiesner does very well, creates an atmosphere surreal in nature. The warmth of the palette suggests a resting place that's safe. And the trancelike stare of the boy tells us that he is most certainly floating between worlds, making us want to turn the page immediately to find out what on earth happens next. It is a "what if?" kind of scenario that fires the imagination.

For Wiesner the process of making a book always begins with a question or concept, explored in small drawings and notes in a sketchbook. This is the "writing" stage for Wiesner. In these small drawings, the entire book is conceived as a whole. In fact, all the initial decisions and overall design happens here. The dummy is the next step. Even if it has to go through changes or revisions, Wiesner doesn't do a second dummy but forges ahead to the finished drawings. If a drawing isn't working but he likes parts of it, he traces the appropriate parts and transfers them to another sheet of paper.

Once the material has been researched, models found, and the final drawings completed, Wiesner uses tracing paper to transfer the drawings to watercolor paper so he can begin painting. It's essential that all the details are in place before the painting begins. The information must be checked, the characters well-established, and their expressions defined. With all the major decisions made, he can fully concentrate on the painting.

"Once I've determined the story elements, I can begin painting. And kind of without a net, I'm going to see where the color is going to take me and let that happen. I don't like to do a color sketch because it is not going to have any relationship with what the final color will be. I don't want to plan that out; I want to leave something to just the moment as it were."

The finished paintings are done on watercolor paper that has been submerged in water and stretched to obtain just the right surface texture for the medium.

In *Tuesday*, winner of the 1992 Caldecott Gold Medal, once again the medium is watercolor, but unlike *Free Fall* it is applied in a very different way. For this lively tale there had to be a real feeling of nature, fresh air, and countryside. And the realism here

makes the magical event all the more fantastic, so Wiesner needed bold, bright color and light airy washes to achieve the right mood, sense of place, and drama. So, holding his breath, he put down large, fluid washes of Payne's gray, ultramarine blue, Antwerp blue, and Prussian blue. This combination truly stepped up the color, and Wiesner says that the first one he finished actually "glowed."

The double-page spread shown here demonstrates many of Wiesner's influences, from comic books to film. It is almost at the end of the book. The magic has worn off; dawn has turned to clear, bright, early morning light with just a hint of darkness draining away over the hills. All the frogs have fallen from their flying lily pads and are

making their way home to the pond. The continuous background painting shows more frogs leaping home along a dirt path and looking somewhat confused by the morning's events. Three panels picture the various stages of their journey. The panel on the left depicts the beginning of the story, as we see the frogs raining down from the sky. Below them, the crumpled lily pads lie limp and useless. The imaginative tale is completed in the final panels on the right-hand page. The role of the last panel is to bring the action to a full stop, which it most certainly does, as we are confronted by two frogs sitting on their lily pads back on the surface of the pond. The frog in front is the one we remember from the start of this flying romp. Now it sits pondering the day's events, unhappy to be grounded. Behind it, another frog gazes upward, wondering if it could happen again.

While *Tuesday* chronicles a magical moment in the pond life of a group of frogs, *The Three Pigs* goes a step further and reveals many different stories taking place in the white space outside the central story.

Winner of the 2002 Caldecott Medal, *The Three Pigs* is a totally unique approach to picture-book design. The genesis for the book came from a childhood memory Wiesner had of a Bugs Bunny cartoon. As usual, Elmer Fudd was chasing after Bugs Bunny. But this time, Fudd chased Bugs right out of the scene, and there they were, standing in white space, nothing around them. Realizing what had happened, they quickly turned and ran back into the scene. Now, to anyone else, that would simply have been funny, but to David Wiesner it was an epiphany. And eventually he asked himself the inevitable question: "What if? What if the three pigs get sick of being eaten up by the wolf every single time?"

Wiesner's concept for the book was to have the wolf huff and puff and not only blow the house down but also blow the pig right out of the picture. The pig realizes that the white space around the picture is safe, and calls the other two pigs out of the picture to join him.

This double-page spread is of particular merit because it challenges conventional

The prince spurred his steed to the mountaintop, drew his sword, and slew the mighty dragon.

picture-book design. There is obviously a story going on directly in front of the reader—a dragon is thanking the noble swine for its rescue from the knight. Behind them is another story shown in the monochromatic pages from which the dragon emerged. There, we see a bewildered knight wondering what has happened to the great beast he was about to slay. The powerful triangular composition created by the shape of the dragon centers the action. And his glorious color—sepia gray greens and ocher that virtually glow against the bright white background—also directs the viewer's eye to the central story.

Wiesner cleverly uses white space to allow a variety of characters to go in and out of all different kinds of stories. In the bottom right-hand corner, a character from "Hey Diddle Diddle" has joined them. And behind the dragon there are pages from even more stories. There is a glimpse of a duckling on the left-hand page, looking longingly at the scene. Notice that the duckling is painted in the simpler brightly colored palette often

used for toddler books. Because of the different stories and styles shown throughout this book, Wiesner changed the media to reflect the unique look he needed for the different genres.

This last illustration is the cover of *Flotsam*, winner of the 2007 Caldecott Medal. Another wordless adventure, it takes place both at the seashore and deep beneath the waves.

Perhaps the most important role of a cover is to attract attention. The text should be bold and readable, the action it portrays should tell us a little bit about the story inside, and the overall color should be bright and eye-catching. The art and design for this particular cover more than fits the bill.

The bright red background featuring a perfectly centered black circle most certainly catches the eye, even from across the room. In this case it also does the job of telling the viewer that this story takes place beneath the surface of the sea. On closer inspection, is that a camera reflected in the eye of the giant fish? Right away, the viewer knows this will be no ordinary tale. The typeface—embossed in silver with jagged edges—looks a bit like an old log that has been floating in the water for a long time.

Swimming in front of this giant fish are smaller ones, part of a school gazing out at the viewer as they move steadily forward. Where are they all going? At the top and bottom of the right-hand margin, two triangles help define the pointed head of the fish. They are filled with a rich, quiet gray blue that is the perfect background for this great creature gliding past. Of course, the direction suggests that we should move forward, too, and open the book.

Wiesner's art grabs the reader from the cover to the last page. Most often things are not what they seem, and the journey is mesmerizing, so much so that it's easy to overlook his extraordinary draftsmanship, his thoughtful composition, and his apparent ease handling paint and applying color.

The most satisfying thing about David Wiesner's storytelling is that it is always unpredictable—where else could giant peppers appear in the sky or frogs fly on enchanted lily pads or three pigs escape their centuries-old fate?—and constantly challenges us to pay attention. He inspires us to ask, "What if?"

**BETSY LEWIN**
Liquid Thought

Betsy Lewin is a consummate observer and a master of implication. When she walks down a street and sees an interesting figure sitting on a stoop, she is perfectly capable of returning to her studio and drawing that figure from memory.

Betsy Lewin was born in 1937 and grew up in Clearfield, Pennsylvania, a little town nestled in an Allegheny valley with the west branch of the Susquehanna River running through it.

"No matter where I stood in town, I could see the hills and watch the seasons change with a drama unique to the Northeast. From the hills I could see the entire town and listen to its muffled voices: the thwack of an ax chopping wood, a barking dog, an occasional car horn. I could see all the church steeples, the river and its bridges, and the railroad tracks where steam engines pulled long trains loaded with coal."

Lewin's town was surrounded by farms, and so, with farm animals. Her family had both dogs and cats, but Lewin secretly yearned for a lion cub or a baby elephant. Wild animals fascinated her. Is it any wonder that this prolific illustrator revels in the antics of all kinds of animals from cats to camels, blue-footed boobies to hippos, and of course, cows that type to determined pigs like Dumpy La Rue?

The pace of life was slow and easy in her small town, and for Lewin and her friends there were plenty of things to do and explore. When she was alone, her imagination did the rest. Often she was Robin Hood galloping through Sherwood Forest or a pirate swinging through the yardarms, and then there was the day when she found the exact tree where Pooh Bear lived. Hers was also the generation that first embraced Walt Disney's Mickey

Mouse, Donald Duck, Thumper, and Bambi. And for Lewin, Snow White in particular had a huge impact.

"Oh, the witch was terrifying, and the deep, dark woods with trees like ghostly people with snatching fingers. It was truly mysterious and pure magic."

These old-fashioned stories instilled in Lewin a gentle humor and a friendly happy-ending kind of philosophy. They also captured the sense of magic she experienced playing in her own woods and fields. The strong imagery of these old films in lush Technicolor would leave a lasting impression that is echoed in her work. The scary parts are there, too, as in *What If the Shark Wears Tennis Shoes?* by Winifred Morris or *Jim Hedgehog and the Lonesome Tower* by Russell Hoban, although "scary" in Lewin's work is more like a good, loud "boo!" that results in a quick, delicious shiver rather than lasting terror.

She has a great sense of humor that ranges from sly to slapstick. Her passions range from natural history to the anthropomorphic realization of her characters, who appear convincingly real and never overly sweet. *Click, Clack, Moo: Cows That Type*, published in 2000, is a fine example of this.

In the book, it's another beautiful summer day, and Farmer Brown goes out into his yard to survey his land. All seems peaceful. Big black crows sit in a row on top of the barn, pigs are snorting and snuffling, and ducks are quacking on the pond. And then he hears it . . .

*Click, clack, moo.*
*Click, clack, moo.*
*Clickety, clack, moo.*
*At first, he can't believe his ears.*
*Cows that type?*
*He strides hastily toward the barn, where his worst fears are realized . . . there on the barn door is a typed note with his name on it.*

*Dear Farmer Brown,*
*The barn is very cold at night. We'd like some electric blankets.*
*Sincerely,*
*The Cows*

For Betsy Lewin, these lines of text by Doreen Cronin immediately conjured the pictures to go with them. All the farm animals are endowed with personality, curiosity, and the many other emotions the text demands, and they are all believable. Lewin's bold watercolor washes have a life of their own and are corralled with a spare, energetic black line . . . just in time.

The bold black line is simple and creates a gestured form that depicts character, emotion, and action in a very direct way. The line contains color that is fresh and bright when it needs to be, and often it is loosely applied in a wash technique. Whether it's an outside scene or the barn at night, her illustrations capture that sense of place so necessary in every story.

In the illustration shown here we see the next note that appears on the barn door. It is a perfect example of the choices and challenges that every illustrator faces. The reader needs to see Farmer Brown reading the note at the same time they read the note themselves. If he simply stands in front of the note, the reader would see only his back—and not the note.

Lewin solved this problem in an ingenious way. She chose to show three cows looking around the edge of the barn door at Farmer Brown and the reader at the same time. The cows are totally amazed at the farmer's explosive reaction. We read the note in the oversize manic shadow of Farmer Brown, who is not physically in the picture. By choosing this vantage point, Lewin was able to depict Farmer Brown as larger than life and exaggerate the degree of his fury. His huge shadowy outline is all the more scary for what it dramatically implies. Note that the shadows of his left arm and leg stretch across the gutter, cleverly making the image even larger. The spiky shadow of his hat and the choice of red as the color around him suggest danger. Beware!

Lewin's mother had been a teacher before she was married, and she read to Lewin and her older brother John every night. Sitting on the bed with Betsy curled up on one side and John on the other, she would read *The Tales of Uncle Remus*, books about Uncle Wiggily, and *The Story of Babar*, along with a generous mix of fairy tales. Lewin's favorite book of all was *Winnie-the-Pooh*, with *The Wind in the Willows* a close second.

As soon as Lewin's mother realized how much her daughter loved making pictures, she did everything she could to encourage her. When she discovered that there was no art education in their local high school, she arranged for her daughter to take lessons every Tuesday after school with Nonny Soderlund, a local artist. So there was Lewin in Soderlund's kitchen, daubing away with oil paints and pastels and having the time of her life. One day Soderlund handed Lewin's mother a clipping from a magazine that advertised Pratt Institute in Brooklyn. While she had been encouraging of her daughter's creative side, the idea that Lewin would become an artist was not exactly what her mother had in mind. Neither parent wanted her to be subjected to such a difficult life. They had both

hoped that she might become a teacher, but Lewin already knew that she would become an artist. In the fall of 1955 she left home for New York City.

At Pratt she met Calvin Albert, who left a lasting impression on her work. He taught both sculpture and figure drawing and made powerful charcoal images of nudes that were not only beautiful but anatomically perfect. These large studies were compelling and challenging. The class proved to be a thrilling beginning for a student fresh from the country and eager to learn.

"My figures were not academically correct, but they were strong and they had personality. I remember doing this drawing of a nude woman seated and looking down, and I hadn't put the face in. I shaded it because it was in shadow and Mr. Albert asked me if I had the guts to leave it like that with the face unfinished . . . and I knew exactly what he meant."

Lewin's decision to rely on the suggested form in shadow to fully express the drawing was a pivotal one. She would continue to use the art of the "gestured form" in all of her work. Her spare energetic line is paramount in her artistic arsenal. When asked about her favorite paintings, she is quick to respond that most of her favorite works of art are the first sketches or drawings of the old masters and not the finished paintings.

"My favorite way to draw is with a pen or brush and ink, with overlays of watercolor washes. I may use picture references or pose in a mirror to get a particular gesture, but for the most part I draw from memory and I draw fast. I love the immediacy and freshness of drawing like this. It's like liquid thought. The images flow through my hand and onto the paper almost before I know they are in my head."

When one of her instructors at Pratt taught a class on children's book illustration, it suddenly became very clear that this was something she would love to do.

"I always felt that my pictures were storytelling and subconsciously I knew that I was a storyteller, but in the beginning of my career people would tell me that my work was very sophisticated for children. But I think it has a double appeal and that's one of the reasons I feel so comfortable with it."

When creating more realistic images, Lewin begins with a series of fast sketches and then proceeds to finished drawings. But if she's working in her favorite humorous style, the goal is to capture the very moment of fun and spontaneity as it's happening and to anchor it quickly on the paper. In order to keep the freshness and immediacy of the original sketch, she uses a lightbox to make a tracing onto watercolor paper and then carefully lays down the finished black line. This preserves the original excitement of the first impression so that the finished drawing itself feels spontaneous.

Once the black line is in place, watercolors are applied. Rarely does she work "up" in scale; more often the work is the same size as the book dimension. To preserve white areas or protect certain parts of a painting from her rolling wash technique, she uses a liquid mask that can be peeled off later.

When Lewin graduated from Pratt, she wanted to illustrate children's books right away, but the pay was poor. Because of this, she worked at a greeting card company. Then she discovered children's magazines and began to both write and illustrate poems for *Humpty*

*Dumpty's* magazine. They didn't pay much, but it was a way for her to build a portfolio while working at a job that paid the bills.

"I did a little poem called 'Cat Count,' which caught the attention of Rosemary Casey, an editor at Dodd Mead and Company. She called me and suggested that with some work this could become a book. I was thrilled. The book was published in 1981, and it was then that I knew this is what I wanted to do."

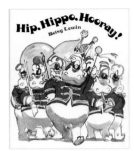

Lewin's editor also encouraged her to keep writing. Next came *Hip, Hippo, Hooray!*, which is now considered the hallmark of her work. Lewin loves to start the visual story as soon as possible. Most of her books begin with a spot or two on the front flap that continue right into the first page of the story. In this case, the illustration for the title page portrays a hippo playing a bass drum as he sets off across the title page, heading straight inside the book. Tassels are flying, drumsticks are circling, and the right foot is actively angled forward. It's obvious that this hippo is on the move. Just a couple of lines and a wash of a shadow define the back foot, which both anchors the hippo and gives him a sense of forward momentum. There is also a linear connection from the bottom of the right heel to the outside of the right arm and across to the outside rim of the drum, ending where the red line stops. This suggestion of circular movement propels the figure forward from left to right. The addition of color in the title page image completes the feeling of the solid weight of the hippo through the chest and shoulders, and the use of a shadow suggests the mass and weight of the huge white drum.

The art for this book was pre-separated. At the time, it was much more cost effective to print books in only one or two colors rather than full-color, and only seasoned illustrators were offered a full-color book. The three colors Lewin chose to work with were black, yellow, and red. The book is dedicated to Calvin Albert, Lewin's beloved teacher at Pratt.

The next example of Lewin's work comes from a series about Cowgirl Kate and her horse Cocoa, written by Erica Silverman. The illustration at right comes from the second book in the series, *Partners*, published in 2006.

Cowgirl Kate and her horse share many adventures, and the partnership between them is one of fun, friendship, and stubbornness! With very few lines, Lewin once again uses gestured form to portray the story, capturing the emotion of the moment perfectly.

This image depicts a game of hide-and-seek, but while Kate is hiding, it's obvious that Cocoa has other plans. In three vignettes, we see the entire story. The final moment, when Kate discovers Cocoa eating corn instead of hiding, is classic Lewin. Even

She hid behind a big tree.
She waited for Cocoa to find her.
She waited...
and waited.
*What's taking him so long?*
she wondered.

She peeked out.
*I don't see Cocoa anywhere,*
*but I do see his hoofprints.*

from the back, it's clear that Kate's stance is one of irritation. With her hand on her hip and her right boot firmly planted, you can see she is upset. Add to that the slight tilt to her head, and the moment is complete. Meanwhile, we see Cocoa with his eyes closed, munching contentedly on the tall, sweet corn stalks. He is in heaven as he turns his head and with a wicked grin on his face exclaims: "My new game is even better. It's called . . . hide-and-eat." Lewin is married to Ted Lewin, also a children's book illustrator and the winner of the Caldecott Silver Medal for *Peppe the Lamplighter*. They met while Lewin was in her sophomore year at Pratt; Ted had graduated the year before. From the very beginning they seemed like a perfect match. He told stories of his family's exotic pets, from Sheba the lion cub to Jago the chimpanzee, and they shared a whimsical off-the-wall sense of humor. They both loved the same movies, longed to travel to the world's wild places, and were dedicated artists. By 1970 they had finally saved enough money for their first trip to East

She followed them all the way to the cornfield.
Cocoa was munching a mouthful of corn.
"What happened to hide-and-seek?"
cried Cowgirl Kate.
Cocoa grinned.
"My new game is even better,"
he said.
"It's called . . .
hide-and-*eat*."

Africa to see the wildlife. This would be just the beginning of a lifetime of exotic traveling and bookmaking.

*Booby Hatch*, published in 1995, was the first travel-inspired book that Betsy Lewin both wrote and illustrated, following a trip to the Galápagos Islands.

"I was struck by the comic appearance and touching behavior of the blue-footed booby. The fact that this species breeds all year round made it possible for me to observe the birds in all stages of their development. My book follows Pepe, a booby chick, from hatching to fledgling to finally meeting Tina, his mate, with whom he performs their enchanting court-ship dance. The book ends with an egg in their nest, ensuring that life will continue."

This book affords a great opportunity to observe the way in which Lewin treats the natural world around us. The pictures are created in watercolor, but without the strong pen or brush line we see so often in her work. Instead they are done with light washes and colors limited to the actual world of these remarkable birds, and the white space here is artfully designed to present the story. The birds themselves are rendered in a naturalistic

way but are endowed with a sense of personality. This combination gives the viewer an extremely accurate picture of these unique birds. The actual courting dance that Lewin witnessed and photographed is depicted with total accuracy.

Apart from giving these dancers individual expressions, often with the set of an eyelid, Lewin simply portrayed the actual bird's movements as caught on her camera, and yet the result is truly comic in the best sense of the word. Once again the consummate observer, Lewin knew instinctively that the real dance steps in nature were funny enough. Here, less is definitely more.

A more recent book, *So, What's It Like to Be a Cat?*, written by Karla Kuskin and published in 2005, gave Betsy Lewin the opportunity to use a completely different style to show us all just what a cat is truly like. The book begins as a class assignment in the form of an interview. The young boy featured has decided to interview a cat.

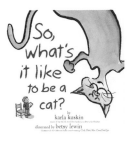

LEWIN

The double-page spread shown below perfectly illustrates the text on two distinctly different levels. The picture begins at the lower left-hand corner, where a small boy in a bright red shirt and blue pants grasps his clipboard with his left hand and holds a pencil in his right. "I understand you sleep a lot," he says to the cat, "but once in a while . . ."

He is clearly anchored to the ground and is looking up for an answer. His interview subject, however, is anything but anchored as he is portrayed leaping off the page in all three remaining corners, and then centered as he flies gracefully across the gutter, a look of pure joy on his feline face. Eyes are closed and lips turned upward in a smile as the tail curls this way and that, creating motion. Adding a touch of color amid the light blue wash in the background are little splashes of pink on the paws and ears.

Lewin establishes the drama here by placing the boy in the lower left-hand corner and making him small and far below the action. But we are right up there with the cat.

Painted in watercolor washes and black line, the white space around the leaping creature also has a role to play. As the blue washes thin out to white space, a sense of real depth is achieved. Together with the quick line drawing of the legs, the feeling of movement seems real and effortless. Finally the cat

I understand you sleep a lot, but once in a while . . .

dives down into the lower right-hand corner, wanting us to follow. So we turn the page.

It's not surprising that when Lewin was a child, her favorite illustrators were Ernest H. Shepard and A. B. Frost, closely followed by N. C. Wyeth, who was responsible for her wanting to be a pirate, and Howard Pyle, whose world of "faeries" and magic intrigued her as she explored her own beloved woods near her home. As an adult, she has also loved the delicate handling of watercolors by Beatrix Potter and the worlds of James Stevenson and Quentin Blake.

Among her favorite artists are Heinrich Kley, Toulouse-Lautrec, Rembrandt, Vermeer, the English watercolorist Thomas Rowlandson, Childe Hassam for his lush garden land-scapes, John La Farge for his intimate flower portraits, and Tiepolo, who was also a favorite of Quentin Blake.

"But I really love their drawings most of all, in particular Rembrandt and Daumier. The Daumier sketchbooks are truly fantastic. They show you the thinking, the excitement, and the immediacy of the line, it's still there."

It may seem a stretch from Rembrandt to Betsy Lewin, but consider the work of Quentin Blake, Arnold Lobel, James Marshall, Maurice Sendak, and William Steig—all masters of strong, simple form and fluid line that perfectly illustrates every word and nuance of the story. Every artist learns from the artists who precede them, and the sketches of these masters have surely inspired many young artists in their quest for immediacy of line.

For Betsy Lewin in particular, the line is where it all begins. The excitement, energy, and the action are captured with an immediacy that keeps her work fresh and in the moment. It never appears to be work; the story happens right there on the page, seemingly without effort. Yet we know that's not the way it works at all.

# HARRY BLISS
## Class Clown

"I was a seriously destructive, foul-mouthed juvenile delinquent. If it wasn't for art, I'd most certainly be incarcerated today." As a child, Harry Bliss spent much of his time making pictures and poring over his own pile of books. Some of his favorites were by P. D. Eastman, especially *Go, Dog. Go!*, and the I Can Read books, in particular those by Dr. Seuss. Then came Babar, followed by Richard Scarry. But the illustrations that made the biggest impression on Bliss were those in the pages of *In the Night Kitchen* by Maurice Sendak.

"I loved the storytelling and the character of Mickey, and I especially liked the surreal qualities . . . the way he just floated out of bed with no real explanation. He was naked, you know, this little kid, and for some reason I identified with that naked pudgy little body. And I loved the way [Sendak] constructed that book—the panels and the overall design."

Born in Rochester, New York, in 1964, Bliss grew up with two older brothers and one older sister. His parents met at the Philadelphia College of Art. His mother did not continue to work as an artist since she was busy raising a growing family. She was, however, an avid reader, and Bliss remembers her with a book constantly in her hand. His father was a "studio man," and together with Bliss' two uncles, who were also artists, ran a graphic design business that garnered a great deal of advertising work in the 1970s. So Bliss grew up in a house where art was part of family life.

Even as a young child, Bliss found himself responding much more to the picture books that were somehow "a little different"—ones that went in unexpected directions or had unusual plots. A few years later, Bliss would discover Winsor McCay and recognize the influence he had played on Sendak, who also loved Little Nemo, the main character of McCay's comic strip, which ran from 1905 to 1911. McCay's sophisticated fantasy and comic-strip format truly connected with Bliss' own interest in applying comic-book simplicity to the picture-book format.

Childhood was also the time for going to the movies. Bliss' father was a big fan of black-and-white movies, and Laurel and Hardy, Abbott and Costello, and the Little Rascals were favorite characters. Harry Bliss loved them all.

Bliss also managed to become the class clown, a title he relished.

"I loved knowing that I could make people laugh—that was huge for me as a kid—and I got to know the assistant principal really well."

Bliss loved comics and collected them with a passion. He first discovered Crockett Johnson from his comic strips, and from there he found *Harold and the Purple Crayon*. The Marvel Comics of the seventies were a huge part of Bliss' childhood. The Fantastic Four and Spider-Man were favorite Marvel characters, and Harry and his friends would ride their bicycles for miles to the comics store to keep up with the latest issues.

Also in the mix was *Peanuts*, the comic strip by Charles Schulz. Bliss loved Charlie Brown and the rest of the characters, and he understood the wonderful sophistication of the seemingly simple plots. That rich black line, the limited color, and the zany humor made a huge impression on him. The range of emotions that Schulz was able to achieve with his simple style never ceased to amaze Bliss. And looking at the work of Bliss today, we can see the signs of this early passion cloaked in a very different style and execution. The simple dots and lines for facial expressions and the gestured forms are there, but Bliss has his own linear style that curves and angles its way from a strong black line to a scratchy whisker on a rabbit. Accompanied by the unique color palette that has become his trademark, Bliss' work is easily recognized. But while his watercolor style is much more painterly in its application than that of Charles Schulz, his humor is at least as zany.

Bliss knew early on that he wanted to be an artist. "By the time I was thirteen I was really thinking about becoming an artist. I was obsessed with the Impressionists and Toulouse-Lautrec, Modigliani, Picasso, and the whole Paris school. At sixteen I started researching Abstract Expressionism. I got a lot of encouragement from my dad because he was a child of the Abstract Expressionists. My father would bring home these flash cards from a board game called Masterpiece. He would quiz me and my brother about famous paintings, and I really got it."

Formal art training began when he was sixteen. His parents enrolled him in summer courses at the Philadelphia College of Art. He became a full-time student at PCA the following September. After just one year, however, he became frustrated because he wanted more emphasis on painting. So he left to study at the Pennsylvania Academy of Fine Arts.

His principal painting teacher there was the artist Sidney Goodman. Bliss loved Goodman's work and his inspired teaching and spent many hours visiting and talking with him. It was a truly magical time in Bliss' life.

After the Academy, he took a few years off—traveling, learning how to play the drums, playing in a band—and then returned to school to finish his degree. Once again, he had the good fortune to come across another terrific artist and teacher. Her name was Martha Earlbacher, who taught anatomical drawing.

"She would say to me, 'You don't want to be a technician. You don't want to be a stupid artist. You need to learn to put art into context. It has to be deep—it can't just be a pretty picture, there has to be more than that.' I really worshipped her and totally understood what she was saying."

During his last year at PCA, Bliss decided he wanted to illustrate book covers. He felt this would be an ideal way to hone his art and design skills. He was a big fan of Fred Marcellino's book jackets, so he chose the topic of American book covers for his senior thesis and won the Eli, an annual competition among seniors in the illustration department.

After graduation he continued to illustrate and design book jackets. He then began drawing cartoons, which presented a unique challenge.

"The cartoons were fun. I had to work out a different kind of line approach and be funny at the same time, not to mention telling a little story. In many ways it was great preparation for children's books."

Eventually he managed to get a cover assignment for the *New Yorker* magazine, the 1998 New Year's edition. It was not to be his last.

Bliss is a relative newcomer to the world of children's book publishing, but his contributions have already been significant. His first book, written by Sharon Creech and titled *A Fine, Fine School*, became a *New York Times* best seller in 2002—a rare achievement for a first-time children's picture book artist. In the book, the school principal decides that children should go to school 365 days a year, and in the hands of Bliss the ensuing mayhem is documented wonderfully. Full of the kind of rapscallion humor kids love, the pacing keeps the story moving forward to its final destination, where the natural balance of the original school routine is happily restored. In terms of illustration, what makes these pictures so memorable is the way Bliss tells the story. The pictures have an overall warm glow that is timeless and universal.

The jacket illustration sets the tone for what lies ahead. The strong underlying design here is a triangle that directs the eye to the title. The title itself takes up the top third of the page, leaving the lower portion to feature the action. A warm brick red colors the title. This red is in turn on a yellow background, outlined in black ink. The yellow makes the title pop and attracts our attention. The background is pure white, a favorite of this artist. Nothing interferes with the image.

The young girl in the picture wears a worried expression as she struggles valiantly to stay upright, but the weight of her backpack is too much. The enormous backpack is stuffed full and covered with stickers proclaiming the extraordinary schedule required by the school. Bliss makes excellent use of sticky notes to portray the kind of life a student would have at the Fine, Fine School, such as, *Big test Monday*, and next to it, *Even bigger test Tuesday*, and then *Massive test on your birthday*, and just above it, *Apply to college*. Helping to hold up the back-pack is a young boy leaning hard into his task, his eyes closed in concentration, his shoelaces untied. Also halfheartedly helping is a dog, reading a book with the title *Unleashed*. Even the dog is caught up in this frenzy of learning. The overall palette is well-balanced and rich in color. The path is easily defined with a long horizontal line of soft green watercolor grass, which is under a lavender shadow cast by the large brown villain of the piece. And notice that the right leg of the young girl moves forward and off the page, suggesting that we, too, should follow her right into the book.

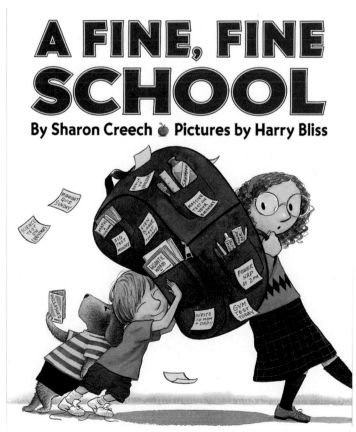

The spread shown here is a good example of Bliss' ability to extend the text and bring his own unique sensibility to the story. There are sight gags everywhere. From the sign above the door, ART IS SMART, to a student holding a book called *The Isms* and a girl and boy sharing a book about Picasso (complete with a fine little portrait of the artist as a young man), we understand that this art classroom takes its role seriously. Meanwhile, the boy holding his half of the book sits with his head way over on his shoulder, looking perhaps for a clue to a Cubist painting (not to mention looking a little abstract himself).

On the table before him is a book on the Dadaist artist Marcel Duchamp. In the corner, three smaller kids are building a dinosaur with the words *I luv Art* scrawled on the front.

The medium here is pure watercolor, painted on 90-pound cold-pressed paper, wetted down and stretched on wooden canvas stretchers. This technique not only helps the color to dry more quickly, it also permits the artist to see through the paper on a light box if needed. The more delicate line work is drawn with a Rapidograph pen, while the thicker black line used throughout is created by brush and black India ink. The line work is reminiscent of Charles Schulz and *Peanuts* but is lovingly adapted to a different style and technique that ends up being pure Bliss—no pun intended.

Mr. Keene was a principal who loved his school. Every morning he strolled down the hallway and saw the children in their classes. He saw them learning shapes and colors and numbers and letters. He saw them reading and writing and drawing and painting. He saw them making dinosaurs and forts and pyramids.

"Oh!" he would say. "Aren't these fine children? Aren't these fine teachers? Isn't this a fine, fine school?"

Another influence on Bliss' work is his son, Alex. Alex also loves to draw, and both father and son enjoy ice hockey, with Alex tending goal. Bliss also travels all over the country visiting schools, which keeps him in touch with kid-speak and kids' quirky humor. This insider knowledge became especially invaluable as he tackled his second book. Written by William Steig, *Which Would You Rather Be?* provided Bliss with his first major illustration challenge.

"A stick or a stone? A cat or a dog? Rain or snow?"

Even his comfort with kids couldn't help Bliss find a way into this sophisticated manuscript. After weeks of agonizing, the penny dropped. If someone is asking questions, someone else has to supply the answers. After auditioning several animals, a white rabbit got the starring role.

Finally (and perhaps with a little help from the class clown), the sketches began. In the illustrations shown on the next page, we see how this artist's love of cartoons and animation played a major role in helping to break the visual code of this text. A simple white background featuring a short line of text and strong narrative visuals is the essence of any good cartoon. Recognizing these concepts, the artist's strong sense of design and pacing kicked in to set the action in motion. You literally have to turn the page to find out the answer.

Again, the art was created using a brush and watercolor as well as a Rapidograph with black India ink for sharp linear details, as in the outline of rabbit's fur.

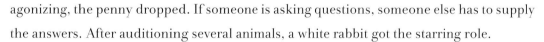

On the left-hand page of the first spread shown here, we see a ginger cat emerging with a bone in his mouth from a black top hat. He looks very pleased with himself. On the right-hand page of that spread, a dog comes leaping out of the same hat in hot pursuit of the cat, his pink tongue swept to one side in the excitement. He can almost taste that bone! Meanwhile, the cat is fast disappearing at the top right-hand corner of the page and the bone is falling into space.

Slight shifts in line change the emotions on the faces of the characters, and the girl's hand gesture tells us first of all, that she likes cats. But on the next page, the second spread shown here, she gets ready for the dog . . . just in case! Subtleties are all important. A slight tilt to the head or a change in the mouth helps tell the story. But we have no idea what the answer might be . . . until we turn the page.

There it is: The girl is cradling the cat while the huge velvety brown head of the dog with a bone in his mouth and his eyes blissfully closed takes up the entire left-hand page. The answer is: A dog! This book remains one of Bliss' personal favorites.

One of the most interesting things about Harry Bliss is that even with his intense focus on fine art, his love and passion for comics, cartoons, and book covers never wavered. To him they were all a part of the joy and complexity of creating art in any form. Now they offer him an enormous treasure trove of inspiration.

His next book, *Diary of a Worm*, published in 2003, would call upon that inspiration and all his skills to create a world that would keep the reader engaged in this unlikely subject.

Who would want to read the diary of a worm? How could a worm even hold a pencil? And then how on earth do you create a cover that's both appealing and able to convey the essence of the story? The worm itself should be on the cover . . . but how do you make an attractive cover with a worm on it?

Well, the cover is where the story begins, and looking at the illustration opposite, all of the above questions are answered in a split second. We do care enough to want to open the book and read the rest of the story.

The first challenge here is scale and the very nature of a worm, but to Bliss, once again the use of white space solves these problems. The first important decision in the overall design of the cover was to create two sections, the top half for the title and the bottom for Worm hard at work in all his glory. He has a definite presence. The choice of a bold worm-like typeface was perfect, and the rich, warm orange color relates well to the mushroom "table" below, visually linking the two sections. On the white background, the title seems rather like a theater marquee in lights, and there directly beneath is the star.

Worm's pencil is securely wrapped in the curl of his tail, and a slight smile curves his lip. He sits on a silver bottle cap (his version of a high-tech chair), and his table is at just the right height. His journal is open flat before him, and he is totally absorbed in his writing.

Note that Worm is wearing a bright red baseball cap that catches the eye, and Ladybug, a good friend who incidentally is looking far out into the white space so as not to intrude, is another bright spot of red. This little splash of red seems like a minor decision but, as it is in just the right place, it's clear that it is a major component of the overall color scheme. If you cover the ladybug with your finger, you will see the exact role she plays. When you take your finger away, notice how all the color seems to brighten a little. The color of Worm was also carefully crafted. It has just enough light brown to create a textured look and a few shiny spots to give him a little more interest. The rich brown dirt below is painterly and works well with the bright, fresh leafy green. And two large arcing leaves on the right-hand side seem to beckon to us. Even the pencil directs readers into the book.

Bliss has mirrored and extended the author Doreen Cronin's zany, witty humor, and the result is a masterful blend of art and text. Worm turns out to be a really nice guy: steadfast, earnest, and hard-working. Who wouldn't want to turn the page, meet his family, and find out what on earth a worm would write in his diary, after all?

By Doreen Cronin • Pictures by Harry Bliss

# DIARY OF A WORM

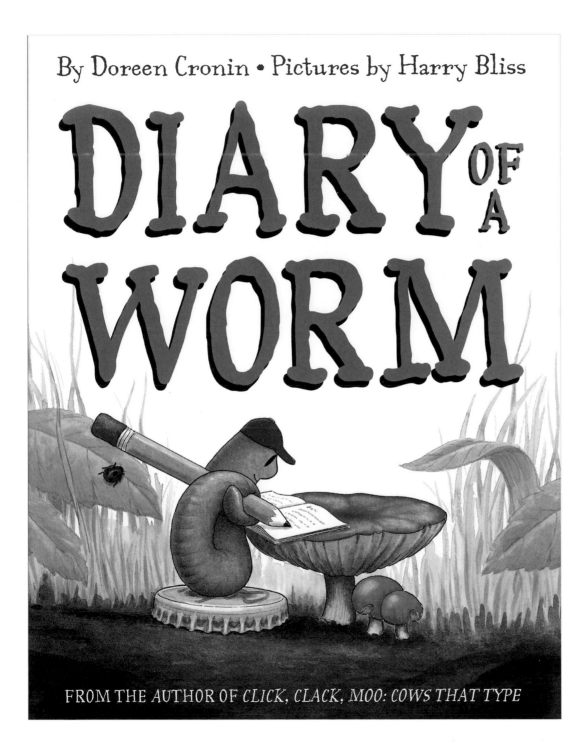

FROM THE AUTHOR OF *CLICK, CLACK, MOO: COWS THAT TYPE*

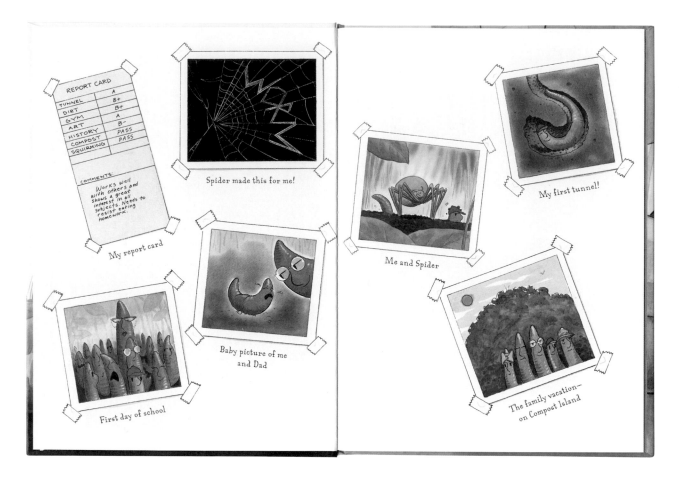

REPORT CARD

| | |
|---|---|
| | A |
| TUNNEL | B+ |
| DIRT | B+ |
| GYM | A |
| ART | B- |
| HISTORY | PASS |
| COMPOST | PASS |
| SQUIRMING | |

COMMENTS:
Works well
with others and
shows a great
interest in all
subjects. Needs to
resist eating
homework.

My report card

Spider made this for me!

Me and Spider

My first tunnel!

Baby picture of me
and Dad

First day of school

The family vacation—
on Compost Island

A story may begin on the cover, but the flaps and endpapers offer two more opportunities to give the viewer more visual clues about what is to come. In *Diary of a Worm* and its companion *Diary of a Spider*, the delightful endpapers introduce the cast of characters and set the humorous mood.

Each picture is barely three inches square and yet contains a wealth of content. Again, Bliss' images add to the story, and he uses both content and composition to gently urge the reader to continue on into the book.

In *Diary of a Worm*, we find a clever homage to *Charlotte's Web* that also serves as a clue that this is "no ordinary worm." That funny image is echoed in the endpapers of *Diary of a Spider*, where we learn that Spider's favorite book is, of course, *Charlotte's Web*.

Also in *Diary of a Spider*, note the illustration of the "neat sculpture." From the tiled floor to the curving, shiny china bowl, the viewer "gets" that this is indeed a real bathroom. But the vantage point is deliberately designed so that we, like Spider, are looking up at this "monumental" piece—we, too, are right in the scene. The warm Pompeian red

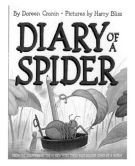

By Doreen Cronin · Pictures by Harry Bliss

DIARY OF A SPIDER

FROM THE CREATORS OF THE #1 NEW YORK TIMES BEST-SELLING DIARY OF A WORM

Cool, huh?

Family portrait

My first web

My favorite book, Charlotte's Web

Discovered this neat sculpture!

Fly's little sister, Maggot

Baby picture of me and Grampa

covers the wall and sets off the "sculpture," and the textured bath rug helps anchor the foreground.

Looking back on Bliss' childhood of comics, old movies, and flash cards, it's not surprising that he landed assignments doing book jackets. Add to this mix his fine-art training and exposure to the likes of Picasso, Braque, and Duchamp and it's easy to understand his ability to take on the intellectual challenge of a *New Yorker* cover or cartoon. This background, for anyone who wanted a career in illustration of any kind, was quite phenomenal, but for children's books it was a perfect match. The class clown has now found an opportunity to stay in business.

# DAVID SHANNON
## Oh, No!

The "original" *No, David!* created by Shannon when he was five.

David Shannon loved art from the very start. From the moment he could hold a crayon, he loved color. His father, a doctor, noticed this and bought him an acrylic paint set. By the time Shannon was five he had made his first little book. It was called *No, David!*

Born in Spokane, Washington, in 1959, Shannon was an active child, although he also loved quietly reading and making pictures of the things he read about.

"I spent a lot of time outside. Spokane has four very definite seasons, with snow in winter and a nice long hot summer to swim in, and I was a Boy Scout. I played a lot of outdoor sports, but I loved baseball best. I was growing up at the edge of where a lot of development was going on, so there were bike trails all over and a swamp, and there was plenty of stuff to do. I loved to bike, so it was great. I still ride my bike a lot."

His love of activity and his childhood memories frequently reveal themselves in Shannon's work. In *Duck on a Bike*, published in 2002, his comic genius is fresh and immediate. And he clearly captures the visual vantage point of a child.

"My dad would bring home these boxes of paper from the hospital for me to draw on. The paper was used to wrap X-ray film, and it came in sheets that were actually folded in the middle so when you opened them up it was just like a double-page spread. And you know I never minded being sent to my room—it was the best place because I always loved to draw so much, I mean I used to draw all the time. In fact, I drew these great panoramic epic battle scenes around castles, but few of those survived because as each person got killed they got scribbled out, so you could end up with a whole bunch of scribbles."

In high school Shannon was lucky to have had a really good art teacher who recognized his talent and encouraged him. The summer he was fifteen, he attended a cartooning workshop in Bellingham, Washington. It was there he realized how many different types of illustration there were. He became especially interested in comic books and was able to take classes drawing in that genre. Even then he loved the storytelling aspect of comics, the way they move the action forward frame by frame.

At nineteen he enrolled at Art Center College of Design in Pasadena, California, where he was surrounded by students with an average age of twenty-six. A lot of them had already gained degrees in art and were now seriously pursuing their careers.

"When I went to Art Center it was really hard, because in high school I had been the kid who did the Christmas mural and the yearbook and worked on the school newspaper, but there I wasn't the Art Star anymore. Frequently when all our work was lined up on the critique rail, mine was the worst."

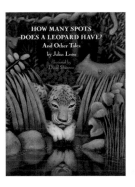

After graduating from Art Center, Shannon moved to New York to pursue his interest in editorial illustration. The opportunity to do a children's book happened by accident when editor Jean Feiwel of Scholastic called. She had seen an illustration Shannon had done for the *New York Times Book Review* and asked if he would be interested in illustrating a book of African and Jewish folktales, written by Julius Lester. That book, *How Many Spots Does a Leopard Have?*, was published in 1989.

The jacket of this book is especially notable for its quiet elegance and primitive styling. The color is true to nature but has a glow to it that is mesmerizing. The glorious creatures possess a personality that is compelling. The cover image calls out for attention the way every jacket should.

To add to the flavor of the book, Shannon decorated all the initial letters opening each chapter in black-and-white, and added a series of wonderful vignettes, also in black-and-white.

"I was excited to do this book, and when the book came out, other people saw it and started sending me manuscripts. I had no idea there was such a great variety and such quality to be found in children's books.

"Then I realized that this is what I had been working toward my whole life. I mean that's what I liked doing when I was a kid—reading books and then drawing pictures of what I imagined from those books. Sometimes it takes a while to realize what it is you really want to do."

When he was young, Shannon's favorite stories included Dr. Seuss' *The 500 Hats of Bartholomew Cubbins*, *The Boy's King Arthur* by Sidney Lanier with illustrations by N. C. Wyeth, and the works of Charles Dickens—especially *Great Expectations*, but also *Oliver Twist* and *A Tale of Two Cities*. It's not surprising that David Shannon is a Dickens fan. Dickens truly understood the human condition and chronicled it superbly, especially when it concerned young children. One of the things that make the David books so real is their profound sense of humanity as emotions run wild and situations get out of hand. But amid the raucous antics we always find tenderness and humor.

In the picture shown below from *No, David!*, we can already imagine what might be ahead, and by the end of the book we realize the depth and range of human emotions that propel this story to its conclusion.

As we look at the pictures in this book, we're not just looking at them, we are looking into them, to find the story. How does color set the mood and emotion? Is the line bold, pointed, sharp-edged, and energetic for action? Or is it thin, curving, and subtle for quiet motion or stillness?

These choices affect our perception of the scene. As does the overall composition of the picture. There will be signs of direction, perhaps moving left to right to keep the pages turning. Or at an important moment in the story, notice how the composition may be designed to stop the action right there and cause the reader to pause just a moment.

The scale in this double-page spread invites us in; we are in fact in the front row just waiting to duck. The orange-red wall behind David is a sure sign of impending doom. Shannon has purposely posed David's bat in midair, a wicked grimace on his face and his right hand poised to toss the baseball. And, judging from the length of the bat, we can tell that as he swings forward it will fly across the gutter of the book and hit the glass clock, the vase, the little dancing figurine, and heaven only knows what else! The swinging pendulum of the clock in the background suggests that it's only a matter of time.

"Tension, drama, and foreseeable aftermath" should be engraved on David Shannon's calling card. He is a master of the story "about to happen"—complete with all the visual clues that show and tell us that it will.

The medium here is acrylic paint, used in conjunction with Prismacolor pencils for the line work. It is a medium that is favored by many artists for its quick drying time, bold color, and the ease with which corrections can be made.

The color itself is a powerful vehicle for Shannon to illustrate every emotion, from fear to happiness, exuberance to impending disaster. The shaggy texture of the carpet showing through the glass table and the patterning on the sofa both seem soft and cozy, but somehow one's eye keeps going back to that red-for-danger wall behind him and the small circle of a baseball that will change everything. The choice of the full-page bleed here is important, too, because it allows a broad range for action and places the viewer right in the scene.

Also, without the confining rectangle of a containing line around each picture, there is much more freedom for the viewer to imagine what might be happening just off the page.

For this small boy, who is always getting into trouble and seems never able to do things right, the last page, shown here, is the perfect ending. We see the comforting midsection of Mother as she nestles David to her bosom and says, "Yes, David . . . I love you!" Again, the viewer is right there with him. We, too, are part of the embrace. And we know that in the end everything will be okay. Dickensian indeed.

Anne Bonney          Mary Reade

*The Ballad of the Pirate Queens* by Jane Yolen, published in 1995, was a big departure for Shannon because the audience for this title was a little older, and the story itself was historical in nature, taking place in the 1700s.

The display type was hand lettered by Shannon, and the front matter and the last page are all created on a light yellow parchment–like background, in black ink with a hand–drawn frame decorated with skulls and a cherubic angel with wings.

The story is about two women who sailed with "Calico Jack" Rackham and his pirate crew and were left to defend the ship while all the men were drinking and carousing below. Painted in acrylic, these pictures show David Shannon's admiration for N. C. Wyeth, but at the same time they portray his own unmistakable form and palette.

When I mentioned this to Shannon, he just laughed and said, "Well, you can tell it's David Shannon because it's not as good as N. C. Wyeth."

It's this kind of instant humor and gentle humility that gives this illustrator the ability to tackle so many different kinds of stories with genuine enthusiasm.

The full-page painting shown at left depicting the two heroines of this story is artfully composed to give the characters a compelling presence. We are placed firmly below the gunwale of the ship while they stand on deck towering above us. Mary Reade has her left hand wrapped around a rope from the rigging, while Anne Bonney leans her left elbow on Reade's shoulder, her hand relaxed downward in a rather feminine gesture for the posed bravado of these two capable-looking pirates. Viewers can easily see they are stalwart friends. The feeling of this picture is colorful but somewhat foreboding. The sky is dark and threatening, with strong white clouds building upward, and the characters are bundled up against the wind that we can see is blowing their clothes and curling a rope behind them. Mary Reade sports a bright red head scarf and sash. The only other piece of bright color is the blue of Anne Bonney's scarf. Both have muskets; in fact, Reade has two of them wedged in her shoulder harness. And the upward tilt of the ship's rail seems to suggest the lift of the waves below to be followed all too soon by the crashing descent. The mood of this picture has been well established, and we turn the page with some apprehension of things to come.

Apprehension and fear as handled in *The Ballad of the Pirate Queens* translate into an entirely different story and format as we enter a farmyard where a happy duck gets to ride a bike. And whereas it's clear that hours of careful research went into the previous book, here one can sense images just tumbling out of Shannon's imagination and landing right on the page, they're so fresh and spontaneous.

Once again the full-bleed design of this double-page spread works perfectly for the expanding action of this scene. The back wheel of the bright red bike is noticeably smaller, which directs the eye forward and upward to the strong thrust of the crossbar and the huge front wheel that is on its way right across the gutter.

We are part of the story. Duck at the handlebars is king; his smile is confident and his right leg, firmly planted on the pedal, prepares to push down hard. Notice the toes slightly curled, just in case. As would be in real life, Shannon has been careful to bring the left leg up and away from that pedal, since Duck really is a little small for this particular bike. It's this kind of attention to detail that makes

the book so much fun and completely believable. All the animals look exactly like themselves, exaggerated in the tradition of Beatrix Potter, who always made sure that Peter was a rabbit first and a little boy second. Meanwhile, terrified Chicken is almost in our laps.

Children especially will love these pictures because once again the art has been created exactly from their vantage point, and they will be jumping out of the chicken's way as fast as they can. Still, the bright blue sky overhead and green fields in the distance tell us it's a beautiful day down on the farm, and they give the viewer reassurance that everything will all work out in the end.

When David Shannon illustrates another author's text, a lot of very different decisions come into play.

Duck rang his bell as he rode toward Chicken.
"Hello, Chicken!" said Duck.
"Cluck! Cluck!" said Chicken. But what she thought was,
"Watch where you're going, Duck!"

"What I look for first is whether it has good images to illustrate, and whether I am the right person to illustrate it.... Then I look for that tingle factor, something in the story that strikes an emotional chord. What's interesting is that the more I illustrate children's books, the more I realize I'm drawing the same things I loved to draw when I was a kid. Baseball players, knights, pirates, Indians, things like that, and now with the David books, I'm actually redrawing what I drew as a kid!"

When he begins work on a new book, Shannon reads and rereads the manuscript and then starts bracketing off parts of the story that contain an image or a particular thought, just as he would if he were writing a paper on the story. Descriptive words are circled and main ideas underlined, and then he begins to break up the story into pages.

"The first real challenge is how to tell the story in thirty-two pages, because sometimes I end up with thirty-six or twenty-eight, and then I have to keep making more changes until I can bring it back to thirty-two. Thumbnail sketches are next, and these are just tiny, very rough sketches, and I get a big piece of paper so I can rough out the whole book at once. I use graphite for the sketches and some Prismacolor for the paintings, too—especially in the line work of the David paintings. At that point, it's a bit like being a film director, as you're dealing with different points of view and tone and what the image is going to be and how you are going to tell the story. It's really like a kind of puzzle, because you can change something on page twenty that will affect something on page five and all the pages around it.

That's the fun part—and sometimes I'll do hundreds of those sketches until I've got it all pretty well figured out. Then I do full-size pencil sketches, and even then I am making changes. When that's done, I make a pencil dummy and send it off to the editor and the two of us talk. Then I go to finishes in acrylic."

The idea of being a film director comes up often when talking with book illustrators. The comparison is apt. Both Lane Smith and David Wiesner, for example, studied film and often think in those terms. Envisioning each of the characters, keeping the action moving forward, and finding just the right angles to portray dramatic moments for the best effect, whether on film or paper, are the keys to telling a story visually.

In Shannon's next book, *How I Became A Pirate*, written by Melinda Long and published in 2003, we find a wonderful combination of the David character and any young boy who dreams of riding the high seas of adventure.

As we turn to the title page spread, we see the large figure of Jeremy Jacob on the left-hand side about to charge toward the title and into the story.

This would-be pirate wears blue shorts and a bright orange striped T-shirt. On his head is a carefully folded newspaper hat. His left eye is closed, but his right eye is wide open and focused on the future. Notice that his mouth seems to be suggesting the familiar "Aargh!," the trademark of every good pirate. Meanwhile, his left hand is brandishing a wooden sword that has already crossed over the gutter of the book in perfect alignment with his black left boot. The pose is one of action and forward motion as he prepares to cross the gutter onto the next page. This active composition makes the viewer want to turn the page and find out what on earth is going to happen next.

Shannon's work is always fresh and honest and full of surprises. Imagination ignites his passion, and luckily for us it seems endless. Perhaps the most important aspect of this artist's work is his down-to-earth sense of humor and his ability to juxtapose tension with tenderness and good fun. He makes the marriage of art and text look natural to us, and no matter how much he protests, his readers recognize and respond to his genius. Oh yes, David!

# How I Became a Pirate

WRITTEN BY

**Melinda Long**

ILLUSTRATED BY

**David Shannon**

Harcourt, Inc.

Orlando Austin New York San Diego Toronto London

Printed in Singapore

# PETRA MATHERS
## An Original

One of the most intriguing things about Petra Mathers is that *she had absolutely no thought of ever becoming an artist*, and yet from the moment she could clutch a crayon or hold a pencil, she made pictures.

"I was always drawing for as long as I can remember, but not well. In fact, in school my work was always shown as inadequate, but I didn't really care—I just kept on drawing."

Mathers had no formal art training, but all through her early childhood and high-school years she just continued to make pictures. Perhaps some unconscious creative force was simply looking for exactly the right moment to find its place. And many years later that's exactly what happened.

Petra Mathers was born in Germany in 1945 in a small town called Todtmoos, in the southern part of the Black Forest. Growing up in Germany post–World War II, Mathers had very few books available to her. But living in the Black Forest, she was surrounded by nature. She loved the birds of spring and the puddles and all the different smells that came as soon as summer changed to fall, but her favorite thing of all was just playing alone and making up imaginary stories and games.

Many years later in *Kisses from Rosa*, which she both wrote and illustrated, one can see just how important nature is to her life and work. The pages depicting the seasonal changes in the woods have a naive sensibility that rings true to the eye and heart.

Mathers' family moved to Stuttgart, where she went to elementary school, and then on to Wiesbaden, where she attended the gymnasium. (In Germany, a "gymnasium" is the equivalent of high school, and students start there at the age of ten.)

Although Mathers never went to art school, when she was eleven, a friend of her father's gave her an art calendar, and it truly changed her life.

"When my father's friend realized how much I loved it he gave me this little art dictionary. And I learned the names and the styles quickly and found them all fascinating. Now that I think about it, I discovered the world of fine art right then. My parents also had these two heavy books of art, and I was always on the floor looking at them. One was a collection of Rubens' drawings and the other was a book of engravings by Albrecht Dürer. They were simply marvelous. My father, who worked at a champagne company, brought home *Graphis* magazine from Switzerland, and I just pounced on those! Sometimes we would go to the museum—my mother would take me to the Kunsthaller in Stuttgart, and I would pick out a few artists and go around looking at their work."

When Mathers graduated from the gymnasium, instead of going to college she became an apprentice in the book business, working in a publishing company and taking classes in business and literature. This combined course lasted three years, and it was there that she met her first husband. In 1965 they traveled together to America, and they settled in Portland, Oregon.

In the 1970s Mathers and her young son moved from Portland to the coastal town of Cannon Beach, Oregon. She loved it there. She began drawing and painting pictures for her son's room, and in 1973 had her first exhibition at the White Bird Gallery. At the same time she was working as a waitress at the Whaler Restaurant, but after a few years, her paintings began to sell well and she was able to leave her waitressing job. Some friends who were book buyers took Mathers' work to New York and showed it to Nina Ignatowicz, an editor at Harper & Row. Ignatowicz responded with an encouraging letter, and suddenly Petra Mathers found herself poised to enter a field of work that had never occurred to her until that moment.

The year was 1980, and Ignatowicz suggested that Mathers start working in black-and-white because that was what unknown illustrators did at that time. Full-color printing was so expensive, that only well known and seasoned illustrators were offered the opportunity to create in full-color.

This seemed totally unacceptable to Mathers at the time, who replied by saying, "To me painting in black-and-white is like wearing polyester clothes."

At the same time, she had been invited to show her work in a gallery on Long Island. She put together a separate portfolio of her work and took it along to show to Ignatowicz, who in turn introduced her to her colleague Laura Geringer, and it was she who gave Mathers her first manuscript to illustrate, *How Yossi Beat the Evil Urge*. Ironically, it would be illustrated in black-and-white.

Geringer said, "When Petra first came to me with her portfolio, she was clearly such an original, and her characters were so intriguing and well organized that I felt she should tell her own stories about them. She reminded me very much of Rousseau."

In 1995 Mathers both wrote and illustrated *Kisses from Rosa*, a fine example of her unique style. The story comes from her childhood, when as a young girl she was sent to her Aunt Mookie's farm while her mother spent time in a sanitarium recovering from tuberculosis. The medium here is a combination of pencil and watercolor, and the color is densely applied to give an overall opaque look to the work.

The very first impression one gets from looking at the picture shown below is a feeling of coolness under the trees. It may be hot in the sun, but here in the shade of trees

and ferns, Rosa, bare-backed, with her little red shoulder straps holding up her skirt, and Mother Schmidt with her stockings rolled down, are comfortable. Everything is lovingly painted, from the little caterpillar on a leaf in the foreground to the two tiny butterflies in the air and the three hornets on Mother Schmidt's back.

The color in this picture is bold so we can clearly see the simplicity and attention to detail, focusing on the small things in life that really matter. The red-and-white-spotted mushrooms in the foreground immediately anchor the eye, so we start to look at this scene from front to back. In the distance, tiny dots of white sheep graze a faraway hillside. A blue, cloudless sky fills the background, and the gentle triangular sloping of the hills brings the eye to the center of the picture.

Although the technique is naive in style, there is a feeling of deep space through the trees to the distant skyline created by the patches of open space, one leading to another.

American Primitive art is an early visual art form that documented rural life throughout America's vast farmlands and produced extraordinary portraits of the people of that time. The color was bold and largely true to nature, and the often simple drawing style had great strength and visual storytelling ability. Grandma Moses' work is a well-known example. This style is a perfect choice to illustrate the simple life in the country on a small farm in the 1940s. More important, the pictures totally capture the moment, as we see an eager but skinny right arm warning Mother Schmidt of the hornets on her back.

In the Lottie books, which she also wrote, Mathers worked closely with her editor and mentor Anne Schwartz, of Atheneum Books for Young Readers. Here we see a very different style executed with an entirely different palette. The color here is brighter and full of light, and the characters are all anthropomorphized in a more sophisticated way. Buildings and various other shapes and forms are lightly drawn and carefully outlined, and the pictures are presented on the page without great depth or complexity.

Not unlike Beatrix Potter's sound reasoning for making the size of the Peter Rabbit books suitable for small hands, Mathers created these books to be horizontal and just small enough for young readers to hold comfortably. The somewhat comic-book layout is also extremely inviting for this audience.

The stories all take place in a little town on the shores of the Columbia River and feature two good friends, Lottie the chicken and Herbie the duck. There is such a palpable sense of time and place here that each story is like returning home to a little town just to see what's happening. And the animals, rather than appearing "cute," are thankfully comic and dear.

While Mathers' ability to illustrate a story in this charming straightforward fashion is powerful, perhaps the most significant thing about her work is her ability to express the intangible in a manuscript—moments of quiet and comfort and safety. Time and place are always well established; we know where we are and how it feels. Indeed, the ability to show us a feeling is one of Mathers' greatest strengths as an illustrator.

In addition to her childhood memories, viewers can also find hints of Mathers' favorite artists in her work. Among the most influential are Milton Avery, Arthur Dove, and Míro. She also loves Giotto for his humanism and Henri Matisse for pure solace. When it comes to shape and form, Hans Arp and George Grosz are among her heroes. But the painters who gave her the most courage to pursue her painting were the Yugoslav naive artists, especially Ivan Generalic, a Croatian peasant. There was a strong familiarity about this work that appealed to Mathers, perhaps because she grew up in the country surrounded by farmland the way Generalic did.

In the Lottie books there are still images of farm and country, and the art is simplistic in the naive tradition, but now we see a more stylized use of the form. Mathers has established a unique style that is a perfect match for the continuing adventures of Lottie and her friends. The humor is an artfully mixed combination of sophistication and pure fun.

The small scale of these pictures makes the art look deceptively easy, but in fact a picture this size presents a special challenge to the illustrator. The composition must be perfectly balanced.

What the text is asking for in this first illustration is a feeling of contentment, and Mathers has given us just that. Herbie is quite happily asleep because he knows his friend will be there at the poetry contest

when he reads his poem out loud. His cap hangs jauntily on the bedpost, and his poem lies safely on his bedside table. We feel his contentment. Beneath the curving, cozy shape of the bedspread we see that Herbie's head rests gently on his pillow. The choice of color is in perfect harmony with the story. The gray-blue tone of the wall behind the bed suggests a friendly darkness within the room, while the small yellow night-light glows with a reassuring brightness. The floor is dark brown, and there is nothing to distract the eye. All is right with the world.

As it turns out, of course, "life is what happens when you're planning something else," and Lottie gets sick and can't go with Herbie, so he has to go through the ordeal alone and does not do well. But when the evening finally ends, he can't wait to get back home and see his friend and tell her all about it. This next picture shows Herbie in his little blue car driving home with a freshly baked cake for Lottie by his side. This tiny painting of a moonlit night with a yellow full moon peering through a break in the gray-black clouds is quite extraordinary. Mathers is able to create a grand landscape in a small space. We see a little blue car, its headlights shining, following a curving coastal road as it snakes around the low dark green hills. In the distance is just a piece of the dark blue Columbia River, with a hint of the moon's reflection on its surface. If we look carefully at the road as it

goes off into the distance, we see just a touch of silver moonlight on its surface as it crests the hills. And as we look at the picture, the road does indeed seem endless, just as it feels to Herbie, who can't wait to see if Lottie is feeling better and to share his cake with her.

As much as Mathers loves creating the Lottie books, she has also found it very exciting to work on a series of picture books written by Lynne Jonell.

*Mom Pie*, published in 2001, is a good example of this series of books. Drawn with pencils, the images are very linear and use white space to great effect. The combination of strong, simple text and a stylized realization of the characters works wonderfully well. Different again from anything else Mathers has done, these pictures are populated with little stick figures and are full of basic shapes. The color is vigorous, as one would expect from crayons and white paper, but what is surprising is the fact that with just simple shapes, such as circles and triangles and straight lines, the action and story lose nothing in interpretation. All kindergartners will surely find these pictures familiar and enjoy the straightforward action and bold colors.

*The Frogs Wore Red Suspenders*, a collection of poems by Jack Prelutsky published in 2002, brings us back to a more painterly approach. Mathers loves to illustrate poetry, and this project was a lot of fun for her since she doesn't usually work in such a large format. The double-page spread shown here, "One Day in Seattle," is of particular interest.

The poem describes a solitary passenger strolling the deck of a ferry boat on a rainy day in Seattle. Dark gray slashes of rain fall across the entire spread, and the background color becomes a combination of the pattern of rain and the lighter gray base tones.

The direction of the rain shows the boat plowing straight ahead into the weather, and the passenger leans slightly forward as she walks along. A large seagull perched on a pylon looks intently across the gutter of the book at the passenger, perhaps wondering why she isn't wearing a raincoat. A bright orange-red life preserver, complete with black safety straps, is the one bright color accent. Without the contrast of the orange-red here, the gray itself wouldn't be so perfect.

The right side of the picture is much more active in composition as the passenger strides purposefully forward toward the gutter. Hands thrust into her pockets, she seems to be returning the gull's stare; the pouring rain doesn't seem to faze her at all. Her face, drawn with a thin line, is a fine example of a simple drawing technique. With just the right curve and a couple of well placed triangles for the nose and mouth, her expression is captured. And the delicate curve to the eyebrow is the finishing touch. Directly above her, another gull flying full speed ahead takes us forward from right to left, mirroring the ferry itself. At the top, a sister ferry speeds in the opposite direction, reflecting the role of ferries everywhere. The large frontal form of the figure forms a tall triangle, and against the half circle of the bright red life preserver, it performs the task of anchoring the foreground. Close to the gutter, one of three fish jumping out of the water completes the arc. It's the one lighthearted touch to this rainy gray scene.

Once again Mathers has established the mood and feeling of the text. The large empty areas and gray palette suggest cold, wet weather—time to go home and sit beside the fire.

Petra Mathers clearly has more stories to tell and illustrate, and a great part of her charm is her unique voice. Laura Geringer was right—she is truly an original.

# BRIAN SELZNICK
## Imagine That

"My favorite book as a child was *The Borrowers* by Mary Norton. The illustrations were so beautiful, and I was very excited to believe that these little people lived under the floorboards in my room. I loved making furniture for them. I made tiny tables and chairs out of spools of thread, and small houses for elves and fairies in the trees outside."

Born in 1966 in New Jersey, Brian Selznick began drawing and making things even before kindergarten. Then one day in school his teacher asked all the children to draw a seal with a balloon on its nose. Before Selznick had even finished the drawing, the teacher and all the other kids had gathered around him saying, "WOW!"

"Even at that age I knew something important had just happened. I didn't like sports or gym, but I think I wasn't teased as much because I could draw. I'm sure I would have been picked on much more if it hadn't been for that."

In fifth grade Selznick was chosen to paint a mural on the classroom wall. He drew a giant Apatosaurus, and within the Apatosaurus he drew circles featuring all the things that his class was studying that year.

"On television there was this wonderful show called *Land of the Lost* about a family that travels back to the time when dinosaurs roamed the earth. I believe I was in sixth grade, and I made this huge tabletop diorama. It had Tyrannosaurus rex, Apatosaurus, lakes, trees, and volcanoes. It got an honorable mention in the Middlesex County Fair."

In sixth grade Selznick began taking art classes. He made drip-wax paintings by melting crayons. He was even asked to paint a scene on the ceiling tiles in his classroom. He started working with watercolors, a medium he loved, and eventually had a one man show at Churchill Junior High that was written up in the paper.

In high school, theater became his passion. He saw a production of the musical *Cats* and became obsessed (which he's slightly embarrassed to admit now). He rushed right out and bought a copy of *Old Possum's Book of Practical Cats*, illustrated by Edward Gorey, and learned all the poems. He resolved to become a stage designer.

He began by studying art at the Rhode Island School of Design (RISD). And since Brown University was just up the street, he enrolled in theater courses there at the same time. But when he didn't get accepted to the post-graduate program he wanted to attend, he decided to travel. Sketchbook in hand, he left for Europe, where he spent a great deal of his time writing stories and filling his sketchbook with drawings. On his return home he realized what he really wanted to do most of all was to illustrate books for children.

On the advice of a good friend, he went to work at Eeyore's, a wonderful children's bookstore in New York City. At the time he knew very little about children's books, and this seemed like a great place to start. Indeed it was. There he met Steve Geck, the bookstore manager who would turn out to be both mentor and friend. Every night Geck would hand Selznick a pile of books to take home and read. Besides Maurice Sendak and Dr. Seuss, who were already firm favorites, he discovered Arnold Lobel and the Frog and Toad books, and Margo Zemach, James Marshall, and Richard Egielski.

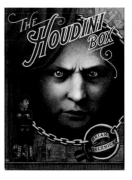

"[Egielski] was the first artist I saw who started telling the story with pictures on the half title and title pages before the text itself began. I also loved Richard's sense of design and the pacing of the stories, as well as his use of frames and borders.

"Eventually I decided to look at a project I did at RISD based on Houdini. It wasn't written for kids, but the main character was a kid. So I took that story and added some pictures and showed it to Steve. He liked it a lot, and showed it to his girlfriend, Diana Blough, who happened to be a sales representative for Random House. And from that connection I sent it to Anne Schwartz at Knopf, and she loved it and signed it up."

Years later, Ann Matthews Martin, who had been a friend from the days at Eeyore's, suggested Selznick illustrate *The Doll People*, a story she and Laura Godwin had written about a little porcelain doll family that has lived in the same dollhouse for over one hundred years. After all those young years Selznick spent making doll furniture and tiny houses for fairies, this man- uscript must have seemed like a gift. The book was published in 2000.

Drawn in pencil, the first double- page spread, shown at right, depicts a cross-section of the dollhouse. By using this compositional device, Selznick literally invites readers to enter the house. This illustration sets up the whole story since it reveals all three floors of the house, each very different in content and decor with neat curtains covering seven windows. Note the clever decision to place the hinges in the gutter.

The drawing here is masterful and shows great attention to detail. Selznick's research of the home and dress fashions of a hundred years ago was meticulous. Even the stairs are carpeted with a floral design from that time. A maid is pictured coming down those stairs. To her

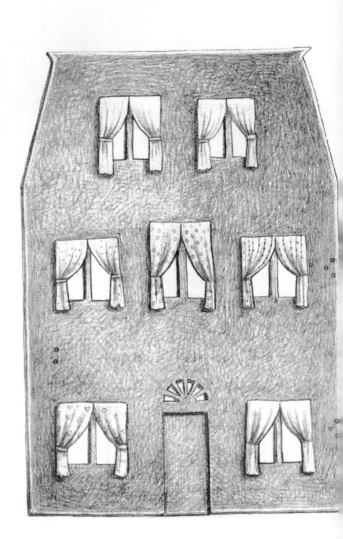

right are two substantial bookcases filled with books, each spine a different title.

This drawing is a fine example of black-and-white illustration. The image has a painterly feel to it due to the way Selznick handled the graphite richness of the pencil.

Pencil can be an intimidating medium, but in the hands of this illustrator we experience the enormous range from black to white that graphite allows. In fact, the end result is rather like working with color, because the wide range of density between true black and a very delicate gray imitates the different tonal ranges found in color.

On the ground floor we meet Annabelle Doll, who is sitting at the dining room table reading a book, naturally (that's what dolls did one hundred years ago). Entering the picture from the lower right is the arm of a young girl, about to interrupt Annabelle. Apart from establishing the reality of the scene and the scale, we understand that the story is beginning, and so we turn the page.

For Selznick the beginning of every story is a great challenge. He looks for opportunities to place a few clues here and there before the actual story begins.

"Every time I start a book, I look carefully for the actual beginning, and sometimes there's a great opportunity to have the story begin right on the flap. I underline descriptions that are specific for illustration purposes, also noting moments that would be great to illustrate, and finding the page breaks that would work for me."

The page breaks are important for an illustrator who loves theater, because it's here that he can set up a particularly dramatic moment or a pause before the unexpected.

"Then I take the double-page spread drawings and trim them and make a dummy book of them. You must be able to turn the page the way it will be in the book. It's akin to cinematic progression."

Cinematic progression certainly applies to many of Selznick's books, which go through many dress rehearsals until he is thoroughly satisfied they are the best they can be.

In *Amelia and Eleanor Go for a Ride*, we can see evidence of cinematic influence. Written by Pam Muñoz Ryan, this magical book is based on fact. As soon as Selznick read the manuscript, he couldn't wait to start. In fact, he moved to Washington, D.C., for six months to do research—and we can see the results in the details in every scene.

"I was so thrilled with this story. I had no idea that Amelia Earhart and Eleanor Roosevelt were friends, and it made absolute sense to do it in black-and-white, especially as Tracy Mack (the editor of the book) had said that she pictured the story looking like an old 1930s musical. So I rented *Flying Down to Rio* with Fred Astaire and Ginger Rogers.

The opening sequence in the book is totally influenced by the opening scene in that movie. This little plane flies right into the camera, and out of the propeller spins the title."

Even the cover of the book is reminiscent of a movie poster from the 1930s. Amelia and Eleanor look dashingly heroic and are featured dead center, surrounded by stars in a V-shaped ray of bands that could be searchlights.

As we turn the silvery purplish endpapers, the story begins: On April 20, 1933, Amelia and her husband, G. P. Putnam, were invited to stay at the White House since Amelia was in Washington to give a speech to the Daughters of the American Revolution. At dinner Amelia was asked what it was like to fly at night, and as a result she offered to take the first lady, Eleanor Roosevelt, for a flight right after dinner. Despite the efforts of the Secret Service to stop this seemingly crazy idea, Eleanor and Amelia jumped in a car and drove to the airport.

The double-page spread shown here is realized from the vantage point of another passenger: the reader. Sitting directly behind the two women, we are indeed right there. The curve of the windscreen defines the cockpit and creates an intimacy. We see Amelia, scarf around her neck and with a boyish haircut, at the controls. Separating the two figures is the control panel of the plane, reminding us that this heavy, solid steel machine is airborne in the ethereal night sky. Both characters look straight ahead, the black night blanketed with a curtain of stars. Amelia has turned off the lights so they are for one moment in time a small part of it all. To the right of the gutter, Eleanor is dressed in a familiar hat, an elegant fur-trimmed collar on her patterned wool coat, and her hair is swept neatly over her ears. Even from the back, her very slight head gesture suggests a smile. And behind her, the doorway provides a wall for the text which is dropped out in white so it is easy to read. "It's like sitting on top of the world!"

"How amusing it is to see a girl in a white evening dress and high-heeled shoes flying a plane!" Eleanor said.

Amelia laughed as she made a wide sweep over Washington, D.C., and turned off all the lights in the plane.

Out the window, the Potomac River glistened with moonshine. The capitol dome reflected a soft golden halo. And the enormous, light-drenched monuments looked like tiny miniatures.

Soon the peaceful countryside gave way to shadowy woodlands. The Chesapeake Bay became a meandering outline on the horizon. And even though they knew it wasn't so, it seemed as if the plane crawled slowly through starstruck space.

Eleanor marveled, "It's like sitting on top of the world!"

While he was considering what medium to use for the illustrations in this book, Selznick realized that even though the movies of the time were in black-and-white, all the stars had a really glamorous aura. Looking at still photographs, he detected a slight touch of purple to the black. So along with a regular pencil and a true-black pencil, he started experimenting with a purple pencil. Suddenly the pictures took on an extra glamour and richness just perfect for the story.

In Selznick's next book we see just what this illustrator can do with full color. A major departure in subject matter, technique, and medium, *The Dinosaurs of Waterhouse Hawkins*, by Barbara Kerley, won a Caldecott Honor in 2002. "It's about

[Benjamin Waterhouse Hawkins, who] in 1853 built the first life-size sculptures of dinosaurs before most people had ever heard the word *dinosaur*. In fact, he really introduced dinosaurs to the world, and the original sculptures he made in Sydenham (south London) are still standing. I actually went to the Crystal Palace Park to see and climb on them."

Eventually Hawkins was invited to New York City and given the opportunity to build dinosaurs to be exhibited in the soon-to-be Paleozoic Museum in Central Park. However, William "Boss" Tweed, an infamous corrupt politician, was able to cancel the deal, and one night, Hawkins' dinosaurs were mysteriously smashed to pieces in his workshop and then buried somewhere in Central Park.

When Selznick first read this manuscript, the concept for the picture shown at right immediately traveled through his mind. In fact, he created a model of this exact scene that stands on a shelf in his Brooklyn studio. A perfect illustration to end the story, this rather small, quiet moment reflects what the story is about: No matter how many people tear down good ideas, the young will always be there to search for the truth and find the answers.

The top half of the picture is in full, bright, sunlit color, featuring a small boy sitting on a bench in Central Park. This small boy is reminiscent of the young Hawkins himself, who loved drawing animals in the wild. A sketch pad on his lap, he is drawing a bird in flight, looking right at a small bluebird hovering overhead. Meanwhile a finished drawing of a squirrel is falling off the bench to the grass below.

The sky is blue with puffy white clouds, and on either side of this scene two fully leafed green trees bend in an arch that meets above the boy's head. This creates a proscenium, with the green grass below the boy's feet acting like a stage. The lower half of the picture is a cutaway of the earth below, showing fragments of dinosaurs scattered among the roots of both trees. The rich brown dirt is somber in tone, but the roots are a lighter shade and so is the head of one large beast staring upward, perhaps wondering what happened. As we look again at the whole scene we can see that the little red squirrel has appeared to the right of the bench to check the boy's picture. All's right with the world.

In his next book, readers go to the theater—or more specifically the opera—with Selznick.

After seeing a photograph of Amelia Earhart and Eleanor Roosevelt, Selznick's uncle shared a story about Eleanor Roosevelt that happened when he was a student in Washington, D.C. Roosevelt had resigned from the Daughters of the American Revolution in protest

of the organization's refusal to let Marian Anderson, a black opera singer, perform at Constitution Hall. Selznick was so excited that he called Pam Muñoz Ryan and told her the story. She in turn called Tracy Mack at Scholastic. "Since I had made *Amelia and Eleanor* a 1930s movie musical, I knew right away that *When Marian Sang* just had to be an opera."

Again, there was meticulous research. Selznick spent many hours at the Metropolitan Opera House in New York examining archival records and touring the backstage areas. The archival photographs were extremely important, since the old Metropolitan Opera House was torn down in the 1960s. But as excited as Selznick was to do these illustrations, it took him a while to find the right mode of expression to illustrate this grand story. Finally the quiet strength and sense of purpose of Marian Anderson herself would prove to be the spark for his creative fire.

In this double-page spread, the curtain has opened and we lean forward in our seats with anticipation. There seems to be a hush in the house. Every seat is taken. In front of us is the stage featuring a row of red brick houses. A single window is lit. In it stands a little girl. The velvety night sky is star-filled, framed by the rich folds of the stage drape.

In the street below, people have stopped to listen. The girl seems small and vulnerable standing up there alone—yet she commands attention. The lighting is low-key but dramatic.

Selznick painted the pictures using acrylics and an extremely limited palette, choosing a rich dark brown to provide all the shades of color he needed throughout the book. Yet the result is as rich as full color. The limited but rich palette creates the mood for the story. The only time other colors are introduced is when Marian attends a performance of *Madame Butterfly*, and at the end when she is onstage.

Just when we think we've begun to understand the journey of Brian Selznick, along comes *The Invention of Hugo Cabret*. This groundbreaking picture narrative, set in 1930s Paris, is graphic black-and-white storytelling at its very best.

Selznick had originally envisioned a 150-page book with a black-and-white illustration for each chapter. As he got deeper into the project, however, he realized that this story called for a truly cinematic approach, reflecting the very beginnings of French cinema. Determined to tell the story visually, Selznick gradually stripped away page after page of descriptive text. The finished book, published in 2007, ended up being 533 pages long, and with its 284 pages of illustration, it may very well lead to a whole new form of visual storytelling.

The story features an orphaned French boy, Hugo Cabret, who lives in the bowels of a busy Paris train station and is responsible for winding all the clocks and keeping them accurate. But he has a special secret, and when he meets Papa Georges (who is based on the famous French filmmaker and special effects wizard George Méliès), who owns a small toy stand in the station, a connection is made that will change his life. The graphite pencil used for this work is masterfully handled throughout. In the illustration shown here, we see Selznick's remarkable ability to create the deep space of city lights against a close-up of two spellbound children. The composition is powerful in scale yet creates an intimate portrait. Selznick places the children in the bottom left-hand corner to maximize their small stature next to the huge clock face. Above their heads, a white circle of moonlight guides the eye out into the night sky. The feeling here is painterly, with the color ranging from pure white to darkest grey. As the white section of the clock face curves downward, it captures these two children in a moment of wonder.

As is true of many of the artists in this book, what makes Brian Selznick's work so interesting has a lot to do with the passions of his childhood. With Selznick's work, however, we find a very diverse group of titles and a particularly passionate devotion to a limited palette. His interest in theater also steers him to approach the white page as he might a stage.

In talking with this quietly passionate young man, it becomes obvious that he is someone with insatiable curiosity and this fuels his work. One can almost see an idea flashing into his mind, and then up pops a sign that reads IMAGINE THAT! And he does.

# DENISE FLEMING
## Everything

Denise Fleming faces a unique challenge every single time she has a new book idea. As a general rule, most illustrators move from ideas jotted down in a sketchbook to the sketches themselves, followed by a dummy layout and then the final drawings and full-color finishes. For Fleming, however, the process is never so simple. Like other artists, she wrestles with the concept of a book, but then, unlike many other artists, she actually makes the paper she uses to create it.

Fleming was born in Toledo, Ohio, in 1950. Her mother and grandmother were both passionate gardeners, so as a child Fleming spent countless hours working in the garden and learning all about flowers and nature. Today her choice in media reflects her roots in growing and creating.

"My dad had a basement workshop where he built furniture, and I had my own corner down there with my own art supplies. I would glue pieces of wood together and make 'found sculpture,' and I learned how to make papier-mâché, which was great fun. One day I made huge treasure eggs with real brass hinges so they opened. I was always trying different things.

"My mother was at home but was very active in local theater and loved to direct one-act plays. My father was a part of that, too, and often built the sets, and sometimes I would go down and help paint the sets, too.

"I like events, you know, and our house was the only house with an extra lot in our neighborhood, and our neighborhood was full of kids. So we would go down to the appliance store and bring back enormous refrigerator boxes, and we would build elaborate villages. We would hook all the boxes together, cut out all the windows and make them different shapes, and then we would paint and draw on the outsides."

Fleming also developed an early love of animals and would ride her bike around her neighborhood looking for injured creatures that might need help. Any found victims would then be rescued and brought home, where she would patiently nurse them back to health. Fleming had a pet of her own, a cat named Abigail who would eventually find a role in one of Fleming's books, *Mama Cat Has Three Kittens*.

In school Fleming was the class artist. When she was five years old, she decorated her reports in hopes of getting better grades. Her third-grade teacher was so impressed with Fleming's drawings that she suggested Fleming take classes at the Toledo Museum of Art.

"I took art classes when I was eight at the Toledo Museum of Fine Art and I really loved it. Before class my friends and I would wander through the museum looking at the paintings and making up stories about them all. I loved the Monet water lilies and there was a Van Gogh landscape with red dots of flowers in the foreground that always stayed with me. And I found this Picasso, *Woman with Crow*, that was just fantastic. And then there was this anatomically correct baby Jesus that we all found incredible, especially me because I had no brothers."

Throughout her childhood there were books in the house, and occasionally her mother would read to her, but it was not a regular occurrence. Her favorite book was *The Giant Golden Book of Cat Stories*, with poems by Elizabeth Coatsworth and illustrations by Feodor Rojankovsky. She really loved the "close-up artwork," and would realize years later that it influenced her own work as an illustrator.

During the summer, the family often went to a nearby lake with an aunt who had an old wooden trailer there. It was a magical place for Fleming.

"The trailer was fantastic and full of surprises. The kitchen table would become a bed and the vanity [was] in the bedroom. You would open up this little curtain, and there was the toilet. Everything was built-in and everything became something else. . . . I loved that! It was like a play house with the lake right across the street."

It's not surprising that when it came time to go to college, Fleming already knew she would be an artist of some kind. Her school of choice was the Kendall College of Art and Design in Grand Rapids, Michigan, where she started in advertising art but then, on the advice of a teacher, changed her major to illustration. At that time, she worked in pen and ink and in watercolor, and was fascinated with mythology, in particular the stories of Persephone and Pandora's box.

While at Kendall she met her husband, David. They were married as soon as they graduated, and they both got jobs at Designers Workshop in Grand Rapids. There they learned many different building and design techniques, since clients came in with a wide variety of projects to be built. All of this came in very handy when they decided to build their own studios. Fleming also designed and built funky restaurant interiors, including the lamps and furniture. Finally they moved back to Toledo, where Fleming would meet the author-illustrator Wendy Watson.

Although Fleming had collected children's books in art school and loved the idea of illustrating books, she always believed that an illustrator had to live in New York to have a successful career, so she never saw it as a serious possibility for herself. However, Watson was quick to explain to Fleming that an illustrator could in fact live anywhere once she made a few contacts. The thought intrigued Fleming, so in 1982 she took her portfolio to New York and she met with Cathy Goldsmith, an art director at Random House. The timing was perfect, and Fleming was immediately given several projects to work on. The style they wanted was a very sweet, tight pencil drawing with watercolor, and they were very pleased with what she did. But Fleming really wanted to do her own stories. So she and her husband decided she should take two years off to work solely on her own ideas.

It was during this time that she received a flyer in the mail from a local high school that was offering a course in papermaking. It sounded like fun, so she called her sister and they took the class together.

"Big galvanized buckets of beautiful colors were everywhere—purples, pinks, oranges—I got so excited. I felt like clearing everyone out of my way and getting to work right then. Before very long I began going back to the school on days when I didn't have class, to continue working, and then finally my teacher suggested that I go to Arrowmont Arts and Crafts in Gatlinburg, Tennessee. So I did that, and it was thrilling to study with internationally known papermakers.

"Then I became interested in making an image in paper. Now I had no intention of using this to make books at that time—it just never occurred to me. I just loved the papermaking itself because it was so much process and I love learning how to make things. I loved this discipline in particular because it's very physical and you never have complete control over what happens."

Before long Fleming realized she had found the style and method of illustrating the stories she wanted to tell. She decided to return to New York to find a publisher who would recognize what she had to offer. That publisher was Henry Holt and its editor Laura Godwin. Fleming says the moment she and Godwin met and began talking, she knew she was in the right place at exactly the right time. She also met the publisher, Brenda Bowen, that day, and by the time the meeting was over she had been offered a two-book contract. The icing on the cake was lunch at the Plaza Hotel and the opportunity to see the original drawing of Hilary Knight's *Eloise* that hung in the hall at that time. Fleming had always loved Hilary Knight's work, and to have this happen at the very start of her career must have seemed like a good omen.

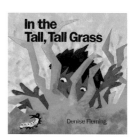

Fleming's first book, *In the Tall, Tall Grass*, was published in 1991. She was now a member of the children's book community and ready to begin work on her next book, *Count!* And "work" is indeed the operative word.

For Fleming, the sketch stage begins with a broad china marker on tissue parchment.

"If I used a pencil I would be putting in too much detail at this stage. I work on tissue parchment because I sketch and I cut apart and then I tape together again to make the images. Let's say I have a little rabbit in the picture, but he's not quite the right size. I'll cut him out, copy the image, and blow it up to a size that works and then tape him back into the sketch. My sketches are like a collage of cut-and-pasted ideas.

"I use the copy machine constantly. Then when a sketch is at the final stage I place the tissue parchment over it and trace the final design in full to work from."

Unlike most illustrators, who would pull a piece of drawing paper or canvas to create the finished piece, Fleming's first step is to *make* the paper itself. To do this, she takes a wooden frame with a wire screen, called a mold, together with another frame that goes on top, called a deckle (figure 1, next page). She dips the frame into a vat of water and cotton fiber. As the frame is dragged through the water, a layer of cotton fiber forms a coating on the frame. The screen is then set atop another vat to allow the excess water to drain off. But even this is just the beginning. Fleming doesn't just make paper on which to put her artwork; the paper is the medium from which the art itself is created.

The work must begin immediately, while the paper is still wet, so the fibers will bond together and hold firm.

To create a "pulp painting," sometimes Fleming actually "draws" on the screen using colored fibers in a squeeze bottle. As these layers are built up, they culminate in the finished image (figure 2). In other instances she may choose to use stencils to create the images.

"Before I'm ready to start pouring the pictures, I've already cut all the stencils. Then I color my fibers so that's all set. But I have to store the pulp in a refrigerator, as it is organic and would spoil if left outside."

Imagine that she wants to create an image of a deer. If the deer is to be behind a tree, the deer has to be in place first. So a stencil of the deer is laid down, and colored pulp is poured (figure 3). By masking off or blocking areas, different parts of the image are created. Fleming describes it as standing in the back of the picture and walking toward the front. This way she knows which stencil comes first, second, third, and so on—almost like a jigsaw puzzle.

To add color, Fleming uses pulp made from cotton rag fiber, to which she adds the same colorfast pigments that are used in watercolor or acrylic paints. Then she adds a chemical called a "retention aid," to help the color stick to the little threads of the fibers.

When the picture is complete, the top frame is removed (figure 4) and the screen is flipped over onto a papermaker's felt, which is a thick, soft absorbent surface with a damp cloth on top of it (figure 5). The final one hundred percent cotton rag paper, complete with picture, now lies on the felt, ready to go through the drying process.

First another cloth is placed on top of the cotton. Fleming then uses a sponge to remove excess water and compress all the fibers. From there the paper goes into a vacuum table that sucks out even more moisture. It is then placed into a drying press between layers of Homasote board, which is made from recycled newspaper and blotting paper. Straps are placed tightly around the boards to apply pressure so the paper will dry as flat as possible.

As we look at this artist's books, it's hard to imagine the laborious process that goes into the making of each page. There is a deceptive simplicity about her pictures. The process is never completely under control. There are so many stages to the process, and during any one of them things can happen that affect the final image. Fleming is the first to admit that this often works to her advantage—not unlike the workings of the Abstract Expressionist painters, who took great inspiration from accidental lines or drips on the canvas. However, personal intuition and years of experience come into play here. One has to recognize the significance of such "accidents" and then know how to benefit from them.

To fully consider Denise Fleming's work, it's useful to see three images that are very different from one another.

*figure 1—straining the pulp*

*figure 2—drawing with squeeze bottle*

*figure 3—using stencils to plan layers*

*figure 4—removing top frame*

*figure 5—releasing image onto felt*

*figure 6—finished artwork*

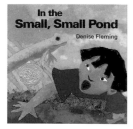

The first image is from *In the Small, Small Pond*, an ebullient, life-affirming book and the winner of a 1994 Caldecott Honor. The full-bleed double-page spread shown here is action-packed and has a feeling of early winter sunlight as blustery winds blow across the water from left to right. Fall has come to the pond. The color here is just right. There is the yellow orange of falling leaves, and a touch of gray in the blue sky.

Beginning in the bottom left-hand corner, three sturdy green leaves bend left to right across the gutter, moving the action forward. On the near shore a small, wide-eyed green

frog has just climbed up out of the water and crouches with its back to the wind. A large Canada goose strides forward in front of the frog, crossing the gutter and flapping its wings in preparation to take to the air. Leaves are blowing, and the grasses and cattails are all in motion. Large flakes of white snow are swirling everywhere. The direction of the composition is tailored to convey the power of the wind blowing everything in its path—we can almost hear it. The large leaves in the foreground establish the scale and anchor the scene. A moment in time has been beautifully captured.

where once
the horned owl hunted
to feed her hungry brood

*Where Once There Was a Wood*, published in 1996, tells the story of a wood that became a site for a housing development despite community efforts to make it into a park. It's based on an actual event Fleming was very much involved with, and she felt a real need to document its passing, while at the same time presenting hope for the future.

The design concept for this book was that it should resemble a journal. The page design is perfectly handled. The images within the book resemble a pile of photographs that has slowly fallen over, the white space growing larger with each turn of the page, reminding us of the clearing that is to come. The angles themselves make us feel a little unsettled, which

is the exact feeling one might have when everything around is about to change forever. The paper is impregnated with pieces of leaves, twigs, and bark gathered from the woods, forever memorialized within the pages.

The foreground foliage anchors the scene, and the delicate handling of color in the dusk is superb as the purple-blue sky fills the background. The full, round moon highlights the owl in full flight as it sails out of the image toward us. We can almost hear the soft swishing of wings in the dark, sad night. This darkling page conjures a sense of foreboding as the owl looks straight out at the viewer as if seeking an answer, or perhaps issuing a challenge.

Like the many young children who read her books, Fleming feels deeply and is curious about everything around her. In fact, when asked what her special interests are now as an adult, her reply is immediate. She says simply, **"I'm interested in exactly the same things I was interested in when I was a kid."**

In *The Everything Book*, published in 2000, the fresh, bright color, coupled with the simple drawing of the children's faces, suggests a childlike simplicity that might be found in a school art room. In the double-page spread above, each of the eight children is reacting to the same thing with a different facial expression. (Rumor has it that the young blond girl on the top left-hand page is Fleming's editor Laura Godwin, as a child.) We, however, have no idea what is causing this reaction. Until we spot the green vegetables.

The use of color here is masterful, since a mix of such bright, strong colors in close association can cause chaos if not handled correctly. But in Fleming's capable hands, we have both harmony and liveliness that's very funny.

Scale is also a trademark of Fleming's work. Much of her imagery is large on the page and presented with a quiet authority. And the full-page bleed format also gives this large-scale interpretation plenty of room to breathe.

Denise Fleming's work stands out in a crowd. Whether it is exploring the everyday world of toddlers or preserving the memory of a lost wood; whether it is creating a visual composition or the actual paper it's made from, it seems Fleming can do anything—and Everything.

### LANE SMITH
### Seen Art?

It's pitch black and strangely quiet except for the gentle hum emanating from the module control center that periodically flashes an eerie purple beam across the small room. A young boy lying on his bed smiles with delight as he silently checks his equipment and prepares for blastoff . . . destination: space.

Lane Smith was born in Tulsa, Oklahoma, in 1959 and lived there for three years before the family moved to Corona, California. Every summer his family would pack up the car and head for Sapulpa, a small town near Tulsa. For Smith, this road trip was truly the event of the year, and looking at the work of this prolific artist, we can see many sights and spatial concepts that reflect Route 66 and the great Southwest.

"The drive to Sapulpa from California was amazing. We would take old Route 66, and I loved this trip more than anything—with its great wide landscapes and little twisters in the distance. And a whole lot of desert punctuated with tacky roadside attractions and a lot of Stuckey's and loads of that kitschy Americana."

Growing up, Smith was a fairly quiet child, tentative in his actions, and although he was quite good at playing sports, they really weren't his thing. He much preferred playing outside, riding bikes, or exploring the foothills around Corona. He was a child of the space age. For him, his backyard was undiscovered territory, and he was an explorer in an alien land. Breaking only for a quick lunch, he spent hours exploring until, forced by nightfall, the brave and weary hero would trudge home once again to civilization and supper. By the time Smith was nine years old, he had made up his mind to become an astronaut.

"I loved the Seuss books and read them all. I was also a member of the library and summer reading programs, but as a kid I mostly read nonfiction. Of course it was the space age, and I loved all that stuff. I did read comic books, too, and fantasy and *MAD* magazine and Monty Python and, finally, science fiction."

At around the same time, Smith's mother became an antiques dealer and started working with decoupage. He watched her create all manner of collage objects, and the house became a treasure trove of weathered dolls, strange wooden gadgets, and fabric remnants. Today it's quite clear that being around his mother's artwork made a lasting impression. The importance of objects, texture, and surfaces are paramount in his work. It's easy to find all manner of distressed finishes and collagelike elements, not to mention the appearance of old toys and doll-like characters, in his pictures. These unusual effects create a powerful sense of time and place. Even his central characters lend themselves to this kind of treatment.

Smith's characters are never "the kid next door"; instead, they push the envelope. Stereotypes need not apply. Pick up almost any of his picture books and you are in for a surprise. *The Stinky Cheese Man*, one of Smith's favorite books, was groundbreaking— there simply wasn't another book around that boasted such a provocative rule-breaking design. Molly Leach, the book's cutting-edge designer, used white space superbly and energized the typeface throughout by varying its size, color, and unusual placement. The type on the title page was huge, the dedication page was upside down, and the type in the table of contents rocked back and forth as the numbers fell from the page. Matching this rollicking beginning, the innovative imagery throughout the book took familiar tales and cast them full-speed-ahead into the future. The book won a Caldecott Honor in 1993. More important, children loved its irreverence and tongue-in-cheek humor.

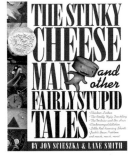

At school Smith drew all the time, but it would take the entire school year for him to summon up the courage to show his artwork to the teacher. During these early years, he discovered and fell in love with Charles Schulz's *Peanuts*. It was a passionate affair that would last a lifetime. At first it was the humor and zany charm of this cast of characters that enraptured the young boy, but later as an artist Smith recognized the extraordinary humanity and sophistication that existed in Schulz's work. Smith also loved the fact that the characters were so simply drawn that just a small turn to a lip line or a shift in an eyebrow could create a huge change in emotion. Occasionally the mouth would just disappear altogether, and yet just the right feeling was still conveyed. Schulz also favored a long, flat horizontal line to present his cartoons. We often find the same long, low horizontal line in Smith's work, perhaps also reminiscent of the flat horizon lines along Route 66.

"Charles Schulz was the biggest influence on my work. More than anyone else. I loved the Great Pumpkin. And through the Grolier Book Clubs I discovered Dr. Seuss, another genius whose work I love. My brother, Shane, was two years older and he had a book, *How to Draw Woody Woodpecker*, and when he got tired of it I got it and really learned how to draw Woody. I was about six or seven. Then I drew Charlie Brown and Donald Duck."

Another influence from Smith's childhood that was key to his visual sense of adventure was his father's job. His father worked as an accountant for Rockwell International, a company that made consoles for NASA. On Family Day, much to Smith's delight, the families of all employees were invited to an open house to see displays of the latest space technology. Smith's greatest thrill, however, was coming face to face with one of the original space capsules that had actually been on the moon's surface. From that moment on, Smith would be forever captivated by the miracle and mystery of space.

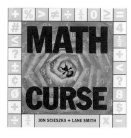

Science, math, and space exploration would continue to fascinate him. In 1995 he illustrated *Math Curse* by Jon Scieszka, and in 2004 this author-illustrator team produced *Science Verse*, another remarkable book that offered good information and, of course, great fun. In 2001, through his illustrations for *Baloney (Henry P.)*, also written by Jon Scieszka, Smith finally blasted off and traveled the galaxy. Many of the characters in this zany tale could well have been spawned in that Rockwell open house so many years before. Leach also continued to apply her brilliant designs to each of these titles.

Many of the pictures in Smith's books contain isolated objects, pieces of machinery, or close-ups of things in cross section that are painstakingly rendered. Often there are also actual fragments of old documents, maps, or newspaper clippings. At first they may appear strange or out of place until, on further inspection, it becomes clear that they play an important role in shaping a perception of time, place, or emotion.

The stepping stone from high school to college came through the help of Mr. Baughman, an art teacher who was quick to recognize the talent in his young student. He encouraged Smith to work on the school yearbook and then to get involved with decorating the Christmas windows in the local stores. Mr. Baughman was also the first person to place an oil brush in Smith's hands. He was, naturally, his favorite teacher, and eventually it was Mr. Baughman who introduced Smith to the Art Center College of Design in Pasadena.

Art Center opened up a whole new world of picture making and possibilities. There, Smith discovered the world of children's picture books. Ruth Krauss in particular was a great find. *The Carrot Seed* is still a favorite book, and Florence Parry Heide and Edward Gorey also remain heroes in his world. Smith's sense of bizarre environments and occasional eerie circumstance bear witness to Gorey's influence. At the time, however, it had not yet occurred to him that he might become a children's book illustrator.

As a student, Smith studied illustration, and when he left school he spent the first ten years of his professional life concentrating on magazine illustration, working mostly in color. In 1984 he moved to New York, and was still doing magazine work but also put together a group of Halloween paintings to add to his portfolio. At Macmillan, art director Cecilia Yung saw these and recommended him to the editors, and so Smith illustrated his first book, *Halloween ABC*, published in 1987. He loved doing the book, but he never really believed he could make a living doing children's books until he got the commission for *The True Story of the 3 Little Pigs!*, written by Jon Scieszka and published in 1989. The book was an immediate success, enabling Smith to concentrate on pursuing his beloved newfound career. He had also found a friend and editor in Regina Hayes at Viking Books.

Smith brought a fresh look to children's books and a zany intellectual sensibility. His pages were designed using the type as part of the art; he changed scale at the drop of a hat; he broke borders when the action overwhelmed the page and needed space. In *The True Story of the 3 Little Pigs!*, his palette was warmly dark and rich—not primary and bright—to suit what he felt was right for the story, which, indeed, was really a dark tale after all. Children got it. They may not have known that some of this art was surreal in nature, but they loved the sly humor and understood the tongue-in-cheek imagery.

Consider the image of the wolf from *The True Story of the 3 Little Pigs!* on the next page. Wide white borders and a hand-drawn line around the art presents this image to the viewer. At first glance it could almost be a portrait—until you read the text:

"It seemed like a shame to leave a perfectly good ham dinner lying there in the straw. So I ate it up. Think of it as a big cheeseburger just lying there."

Then you catch the wicked gleam in the eye of Mr. A. T. Wolf, and notice that his head breaks the upper border as if to suggest that he cannot be contained. He is definitely in charge. He is dapper—he wears a bow tie with ease and a vest that is beautifully painted with stripes to emphasize his height. The extra-small hands, or rather paws, together

with the larger-than-life nose and cheeks are trademarks of the artist, who loves to make small things smaller and big things bigger in graphic statements that demand attention. Although the outcome of the story is sinister, we enjoy the art in an abstract way. Fortunately the wolf's dinner is pictured like a roseate balloon with little hairs and a curly could-be tail. It certainly doesn't look dead or morbid. Notice the textured surface color behind A. T. and how well it transitions into his coloring. The simple structure of the central figure ending in the curve of his dinner below is in perfect balance in the space. This scene is compelling because the composition demands your attention, and it's not just because the head is bigger than the body. The text defines the intention, and the suggestion of a cheeseburger somehow softens the reality.

Smith's interest in easel painting and line art began with his first trip to a museum while he was at Art Center. Immediately after that, he traveled to New York to see the museums there. The artists he discovered and came to admire are a fascinating group.

Kurt Schwitters, a German artist who was a major figure in the avant-garde movement in Paris in the early 1930s and '40s, was a huge influence. Avant-garde art appeared as an immediate reaction to the devastation of World War I. Art began to be created from the junk and trash in the streets of war-torn cities, a powerful reaction against the new machine-age technology. Generally acknowledged as the twentieth century's greatest master of collage, Schwitters juxtaposed the deliberate with the serendipitous, realism with abstraction, the playful with the enigmatic, all with materials scavenged from street gutters and trash bins.

Smith was extremely influenced by the atmospheric work of Edward Hopper, with its superb handling of surface light, long shadow forms, and saturated color. He also loved the playfulness of Paul Klee, the unusual shapes and compositions of Jean Dubuffet, and the imagination and fun of Alexander Calder. The swinging mobiles informed Smith's own linear sensibility and spatial consciousness.

In *Baloney (Henry P.)*, Smith was finally able to blast off into space. It was important to him that the art reflect the space technology that he remembered from his childhood, so the art, created on the computer, was done in a kind of retro 1960s style.

Henry P. Baloney is a small green alien with a swatch of hair that stands straight up on his head and a small, curving body form that is vaguely reminiscent of a distant Earth cousin by the name of Linus. His predicament is that he is late for school one time too many and his teacher Miss Bugscuffle is threatening him with lifelong detention unless he has a very good reason. Of course imagination comes to the rescue.

The double-page spread shown here depicts Henry at the moment of takeoff. Smith uses extremes of facial expression to convey Henry's terror. His triangular body is already pointing skyward. And then he's off into space. There is a great vulnerability about this little green alien. We feel for him because he is a little guy against big odds. We care about him, especially as we see him working so hard to erase

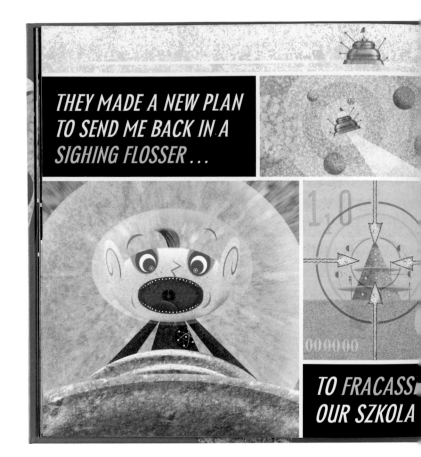

the instructions to the Sighing Flosser (a great spoonerism). The use of jet-black type areas suggests deep space, and the comic-book format keeps the story moving forward.

The right-hand page is a perfect example of a scanned document being successfully used in a composition. Henry's trusty Zimulus eraser creates a weathered surface as it works its way down to the bottom section of the page. The blurring of the eraser top suggests furious and desperate action on the part of Henry P. Baloney to save himself from destruction.

The spread has many different surfaces, from an Impressionist-like background to the flat-colored forms and the plastic mottled gray structure that Henry grasps frantically as he screams at the top of his lungs. The simple, strong, bold lines of white text are also very much a part of the composition. They seem to come to us straight from the black void of space itself, leading us from left to right. And as the eye moves from top to bottom, the frantic eraser seems bent on thrusting us forward to turn the page.

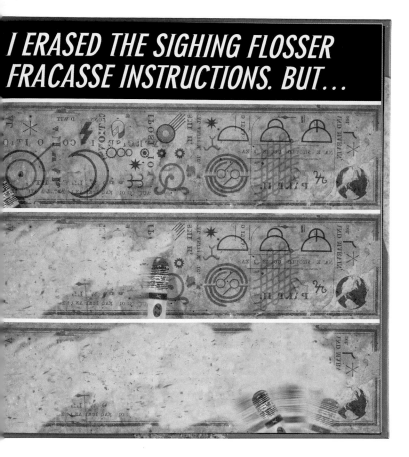

## I ERASED THE SIGHING FLOSSER FRACASSE INSTRUCTIONS. BUT…

It's not surprising that Smith is intrigued by the computer. And as he has grown more proficient with its technology his desire to use the computer as a tool to create beautiful art in a painterly way has grown increasingly ambitious. For him the end result is what it is all about—and that, simply put, is the book.

"There is something about exploration of a painting surface that is always fun. I constantly found myself wanting to experiment when the paint was dry. I'd use sandpaper and erase an area. . . . And then if accidents happened when I was working on the finishes I would make use of them so that they would become a part of the art. Now with the computer, I can create all kinds of 'accidents,' which is a fantastic way to get down exactly what's in my head. But I still want the paintings to look very organic and free-form within that."

Smith's next book—*The Very Persistent Gappers of Frip*, was created entirely on the computer.

"I painted mottled textures and scanned a piece of actual tin. Then I played with the color until it was right, and then scanned in more brushstroke-type textures. Working this way, a lot of bits and pieces come together to form the whole picture. Some are drawn by hand and scanned in, others—like the cloud shapes—I created right on the computer."

The mood of the picture shown on the next page is both mysterious and surreal. The double-page spread bleeds to the edges and is remarkably detailed and colorful for such a limited palette. By mottling the gray-and-white cloud forms and placing a dark gray shape

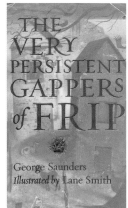

THE VERY PERSISTENT GAPPERS of FRIP

George Saunders
*Illustrated by* Lane Smith

across part of the moon, it emerges as an eerie silver disk in an uncertain sky. And by keeping the palette in shades of gray and green throughout, Smith achieves a sense of conformity and control that plays right along with the strange row of moving men that are marching across the page with the little green shack on their backs. The house is long and narrow, and the roof points in the direction of the action.

The whole scene is once again presented to the viewer on a low, flat horizon line that goes from one side of the page to the other. The wall facing us contains a small upper window filled with yellow light. And there, standing sideways with his head pointing in the direction of the moving house, is a small boy. With a round face and fuzzy hair that stands straight up on his head, his features are small triangles that register both fear and a kind of determination to stand his ground no matter what. No one is going to move him from his room and his house. So he remains standing in his normal place at the window, refusing to give in to the laws of gravity or the will of the movers.

"There's something so poignant about having him be perfectly centered. These strange men are moving his house, and he's staying and not going anywhere. He's like Buster Keaton in all those

old black-and-white movies. He was always the brave 'little guy' in a difficult situation, but he always conveyed a real sincerity and poignancy. I love the work of Buster Keaton."

Once again we find the familiar elements of eccentric characters, weathered surfaces, and a provocative approach to scale. The picture is perfectly composed. The half circles created by the backs of the movers, together with the forward thrust of the movers' legs, warn us that at any moment this house will be marched right off the page. This picture tells the story.

"I've always preferred making books over being a fine artist and doing a painting that would be exhibited somewhere and then sold to a private collector."

Smith loves the process of creating a book. Yet much of the art and technique we see in Smith's books can be traced back to the building featured in *Seen Art?*, namely the New York MoMA.

*Seen Art?*, written by Jon Scieszka and designed, once again, by Molly Leach, is a compact, horizontal book that begs to be explored.

The premise of the story is that a small boy tells his friend Art that he will meet him at the corner of Fifth Avenue and 53rd Street in New York City. When he cannot find him anywhere he asks a lady for help—"Have you seen Art?"

"Good," I said. "I was starting to think I was in the wrong place."

"Oh no," said the girl.
"You are in the right place. You just have to look. You have to see."

"Wow. I—"

"Yes," she said. "Your eye. Your dream can be what is real."

The frustrated search for Art continues on the spread shown here. The boy stands there, totally dejected, with his head down and his tongue hanging out. Right away the body of the young boy and the forward motion of the girl start the movement from left to right.

Featured on this white background are three things: *Object* by Meret Oppenheim, *The False Mirror* by René Magritte, and *The Persistence of Memory* by Salvador Dali. These three well-known pieces are of course in the New York MoMA collection, and looking at the other choices displayed it tells us even more about Lane Smith.

The first thing we notice is how at home these two characters appear next to these works of art. They are both realized in an extremely sophisticated way, and with a European flavor. The hair, perhaps reminiscent of Paul Klee in a playful mode, is also pure Lane Smith. And though cartoonlike, their expressions and gestures come across beautifully. The squiggly free-form line, the dots and small circles for eyes, and the tiny hands are trademarks of this illustrator, and they effectively translate the emotions here. The wiggly little line creating the contented little smile on the girl's face is particularly convincing. There is a little texture in the face and hands, a pale suggestion of pink in the face, and the choice of color for the type and their clothing is in perfect harmony with the art on the page. The white background does the rest.

"What's with the ants attacking the gold watch?

And time is messed up here, too.

But where is Art?"

As the girl points to *The False Mirror* on the left-hand page we stop and look at it, too. After crossing the gutter they both appear larger as the young boy points at *The Persistence of Memory* and asks, "What's with the ants attacking the gold watch?" Again, we follow the direction of the boy's hand and ponder the same question.

Of course we have to continue the story and turn the page, because there in the bottom right-hand corner is the question: *"But where is Art?"*

We may not always be sure where Art is, but we always know exactly where Lane Smith is as he artfully reinvents himself and his work time and time again. The one thing that never changes is that it always changes . . .

He is most definitely not the boy next door, and he has Seen Art.

# ACKNOWLEDGMENTS

In 1964 I traveled with the painter Nell Blaine from New York to London, Paris, Madrid, and Lisbon. We visited every major museum and art collection in each city, and Blaine, a passionate teacher, never stopped talking. It is she I have to thank for introducing me to the world of fine art.

A decade later, working as an assistant art director for *Cricket* magazine in Lyme, New Hampshire, Trina Schart Hyman introduced me to the world of children's book illustration. The next six years were a journey of discovery into a fascinating genre.

In the 1980s, Barbara Lucas, then head of Children's Books at Harcourt Brace Jovanovich in New York, became another good friend and colleague, and, when she began the annual Summer Publishing Program at Vassar College, invited me to speak each year about the fine art of children's book illustration, so I have a very special thank-you to Barbara for giving me a platform for further exploration.

Also during the eighties, Zena Sutherland, a professor of children's literature at the University of Chicago and a giant in the world of children's books, asked me when I was going to write a book showing just what makes the very best of children's book illustration a fine art form. It would take a long time to be given the opportunity and find the right voice. Unfortunately Zena is no longer with us and is unable to see this book (yet knowing Zena I wouldn't put it past her). So thank you so much to someone who was always supportive at a time when "fine art" was not a description given to children's book illustration.

A decade later, David Reuther asked me if I would do a book like this for him at Sea-Star. The timing was right, and I happily agreed. There, under the guidance of Andrea Spooner, my editor, we plotted the book and talked for hours about the central focus and the right voice. Then one day SeaStar went up for sale and everything stopped. But thank you David for getting me to the writing table, and to Andrea, my heartfelt thanks for caring so much about this venture.

Finally along came Chronicle Books in San Francisco, who purchased SeaStar, and a call from Victoria Rock, the founder of Chronicle's children's book list, saying she had just read my notes for *Show and Tell* and would love to publish it. So thank you Victoria for believing in the book, and for working with Melissa Manlove to keep me on track and with Sara Gillingham to help me find the right way to both show and tell this remarkable story.

# IMAGE CREDITS

Page 5: From *Eloise* by Kay Thompson. Copyright © 1955 by Kay Thompson (text); Copyright © 1955 by Hilary Knight (illustrations). By permission of Simon & Schuster. Page 7: From *No, David!* by David Shannon. Scholastic Inc./Blue Sky Press. Copyright ©1998 by David Shannon. Reprinted by permission. Page 10: From *Eloise* by Kay Thompson. Copyright © 1955 by Kay Thompson (text); Copyright © 1955 by Hilary Knight (illustrations). By permission of Simon & Schuster. Page 13: From *Eloise* by Kay Thompson. Copyright © 1955 by Kay Thompson (text); Copyright © 1955 by Hilary Knight (illustrations). By permission of Simon & Schuster. Page 14: Jacket cover, from *Eloise* by Kay Thompson. Copyright © 1955 by Kay Thompson (text); Copyright © 1955 by Hilary Knight (illustrations). By permission of Simon & Schuster. Page 15: From *Eloise* by Kay Thompson. Copyright © 1955 by Kay Thompson (text); Copyright © 1955 by Hilary Knight (illustrations). By permission of Simon & Schuster. Page 16: From *Eloise* by Kay Thompson. Copyright © 1955 by Kay Thompson (text); Copyright © 1955 by Hilary Knight (illustrations). By permission of Simon & Schuster. Jacket cover, from *Eloise in Paris* by Kay Thompson. Copyright © 1957 by Kay Thompson (text); Copyright © 1957 by Hilary Knight (illustrations). By permission of Simon & Schuster. Jacket cover, from *Eloise Takes a Bawth* by Kay Thompson. Copyright © 2002 by Kay Thompson (text); Copyright © 2002 by Hilary Knight (illustrations). By permission of Simon & Schuster. Page 17: Jacket cover, from *Eloise in Moscow* by Kay Thompson. Copyright © 1959 by Kay Thompson (text); Copyright © 1959 by Hilary Knight (illustrations). By permission of Simon & Schuster. Page 18: Jacket cover and excerpt, from *Warren Weasel's Worse Than Measles* by Alice Bach. Copyright © 1980 by Alice Bach (text); Copyright © 1980 by Hilary Knight (illustrations). By permission of Harper and Row, an imprint of HarperCollins. Page 19: Jacket cover and excerpt, from *The Circus Is Coming. . .* by Hilary Knight, copyright © 1978, 2007 by Random House, Inc. Afterword copyright © 2007 by Paul Binder. Used by permission of Golden Books, an imprint of Random House Children's Books, a division of Random House, Inc. Jacket cover, from *Beauty and the Beast* by Richard Howard. Copyright © 1963 by Richard Howard (translation); Copyright © 1963 by Hilary Knight (illustrations). By permission from Macmillan Publishers. Page 20: Jacket cover, from *Side by Side* by Lee Bennett Hopkins. Copyright © 1988 by Lee Bennett Hopkins (text); Copyright © 1988 by Hilary Knight (illustrations). By permission of Simon & Schuster. Page 20–21: From *Side by Side* by Lee Bennett Hopkins. Copyright © 1988 by Lee Bennett Hopkins (text); Copyright © 1988 by Hilary Knight (illustrations). By permission of Simon & Schuster. Page 21: Jacket cover, from *Eloise at Christmastime* by Kay Thompson. Copyright © 1958 by Kay Thompson (text); Copyright © 1958 by Hilary Knight (illustrations). By permission of Simon & Schuster. Page 22: Copyright © 1983 by Trina Schart Hyman. Reprinted from *Little Red Riding Hood* by permission of Holiday House. Page 25: Jacket cover, from *King Stork* by Howard Pyle. Copyright © 1998 by Howard Pyle (text); Copyright © 1998 by Trina Schart Hyman (illustrations). By permission of HarperCollins. Page 26–27: From *Snow White* by Paul Heins. Copyright © by Paul Heins (translation); Copyright © 1974 Trina Schart Hyman (illustrations). By permission of Little, Brown & Company. Page 27: Jacket cover, from *Snow White* by Paul Heins. Copyright © by Paul Heins (translation); Copyright © 1974 by Trina Schart Hyman (illustrations). By permission of Little, Brown & Company. Page 28: Copyright © 1983 by Trina Schart Hyman. Reprinted from *Little Red Riding Hood* by permission of Holiday House. Page 28–29: Copyright © 1983 by Trina Schart Hyman. Reprinted from *Little Red Riding Hood* by permission of Holiday House. Page 30: From *Magic in the Mist* by Margaret Mary Kimmel. Copyright © 1976 by Margaret Mary Kimmel (text); Copyright © 1976 by Trina Schart Hyman (illustrations). By permission of Simon & Schuster. Page 31: Jacket cover, from *Magic in the Mist* by Margaret Mary Kimmel. Copyright © 1976 by Margaret Mary Kimmel (text); Copyright © 1976 by Trina Schart Hyman (illustrations). By permission of Simon & Schuster. Page 31: Jacket cover, from *Saint George and the Dragon* by Margaret Hodges. Copyright © 1984 by Margaret Hodges (text); Copyright © 1984 by Trina Schart Hyman (illustrations). By permission of Little, Brown & Company. Page 32–33: From *Saint George and the Dragon* by Margaret Hodges. Copyright © 1984 by Margaret Hodges (text); Copyright © 1984 by Trina Schart Hyman (illustrations). By permission of Little, Brown & Company. Page 33: Copyright © 2006 by Katrin Hyman Tchana. Reprinted from *Changing Woman and her Sisters: Stories of Goddesses from Around the World* by permission of Holiday House. Page 34: From *Martin's Big Words* by Doreen Rappaport. Copyright © 2001 by Doreen Rappaport (text); Copyright © 2001 by Bryan Collier (illustrations). By permission of Hyperion Books for Children. Page 36: Illustrations from *Uptown* by Bryan Collier. Copyright © 2000 by Bryan Collier. Reprinted by permission of Henry Holt and Company. Page 36–37: Illustrations from *Uptown* by Bryan Collier. Copyright © 2000 by Bryan Collier. Reprinted by permission of Henry Holt and Company. Page 38: Jacket cover and excerpt, from *Freedom River* by Doreen Rappaport. Copyright © 2000 by Doreen Rappaport (text); Copyright © 2000 by Bryan Collier (illustrations). By permission of Hyperion Books for Children. Page 39: From *Freedom River* by Doreen Rappaport. Copyright © 2000 by Doreen Rappaport (text); Copyright © 2000 by Bryan Collier (illustrations). By permission of Hyperion Books for Children. Page 40: Jacket cover, from *Martin's Big Words* by Doreen Rappaport. Copyright © 2001 by Doreen Rappaport (text); Copyright © 2001 by Bryan Collier (illustrations). By permission of Hyperion Books for Children. Page 40–41: From *Martin's Big Words* by Doreen Rappaport. Copyright © 2001 by Doreen Rappaport (text); Copyright © 2001 by Bryan Collier (illustrations). By permission of Hyperion Books for Children. Page 42: Illustrations by Bryan Collier from *Rosa* by Nikki Giovanni. Copyright © 2005 by Bryan Collier. Reprinted by permission of Henry Holt and Company. Page 43: Illustrations by Bryan Collier from *Rosa* by Nikki Giovanni. Copyright © 2005 by Bryan Collier. Reprinted by permission of Henry Holt and Company. Page 44: From *Knick-Knack Paddywack!* by Paul O. Zelinsky, copyright © 2002 by Paul O. Zelinsky, illustrations. Used by permission of Dutton Children's Books, A Division of Penguin Young Readers Group, A Member of Penguin Group (USA) Inc., 345 Hudson Street, New York, NY 10014. All rights reserved. Page 46–47: From *How I Hunted the Little Fellows* by Boris Zhitkov, illustrated by Paul O. Zelinsky. Copyright © 1979 by Paul O. Zelinsky (Illustrations). Reprinted by permission of Paul O. Zelinsky. Page 48: Jacket cover, from *Swamp Angel* by Anne Isaacs, illustrated by Paul O. Zelinsky, copyright © 1984 by Paul O. Zelinsky, illustrations. Used by permission of Dutton, A Division of Penguin Young Readers Group, A Member of Penguin Group (USA) Inc., 345 Hudson Street, New York, NY 10014. All rights reserved. Page 48–49: From *Swamp Angel* by Anne Isaacs, illustrated by Paul O. Zelinsky, copyright © 1984 by Paul O. Zelinsky, illustrations. Used by permission of Dutton, A Division of Penguin Young Readers Group, A Member of Penguin Group (USA) Inc., 345 Hudson Street, New York, NY 10014. All rights reserved. Page 50: Jacket cover, from *Hansel and Gretel* by Rika Lesser, illustrated by Paul O. Zelinsky, copyright © 1984 by Paul O. Zelinsky, illustrations. Used by permission of Dutton Children's Books, A Division of Penguin Young Readers Group, A Member of Penguin Group (USA) Inc., 345 Hudson Street, New York, NY 10014. All rights reserved. Jacket cover, from *Rapunzel* by Paul O. Zelinsky, copyright © 1997 by Paul O. Zelinsky. Used by permission of Dutton Children's Books, A Division of Penguin Young Readers Group, A Member of Penguin Group (USA) Inc., 345 Hudson Street, New York, NY 10014. All rights reserved. Page 51: From *Rapunzel* by Paul O. Zelinsky, copyright © 1997 by Paul O. Zelinsky. Used by permission of Dutton Children's Books, A Division of Penguin Young Readers Group, A Member of Penguin Group (USA) Inc., 345 Hudson Street, New York, NY 10014. All rights reserved. Page 52: Jacket cover, from *Knick-Knack Paddywack!* by Paul O. Zelinsky, copyright © 2002 by Paul O. Zelinsky, illustrations. Used by permission of Dutton Children's Books, A Division of Penguin Young Readers Group, A Member of Penguin Group (USA) Inc., 345 Hudson Street, New York, NY 10014. All rights reserved. Page 52–53: From *Knick-Knack Paddywack!* by Paul O. Zelinsky, copyright © 2002 by Paul O. Zelinsky, illustrations. Used by permission of Dutton Children's Books, A Division of Penguin Young Readers Group, A Member of Penguin Group (USA) Inc., 345 Hudson Street, New York, NY 10014. All rights reserved. Page 54: Illustration from *The Three Pigs* by David Wiesner. Copyright © 2001 by David Wiesner. Reprinted by permission of Clarion Books, an imprint of Houghton Mifflin Company. All rights reserved. Page 57: Jacket cover from *Honest Andrew* by Gloria Skurzynski, illustration copyright © 1980 by David Wiesner, reproduced by permission of Harcourt, Inc. Jacket cover, from *Free Fall* by David Wiesner. Copyright © 1988 by David Wiesner. By permission of Lothrup, Lee & Shepard, an imprint of HarperCollins. Page 58–59: From *Free Fall* by David Wiesner. Copyright © 1988 by David Wiesner. By permission of Lothrup, Lee & Shepard, an imprint of HarperCollins. Page 60: Jacket cover, from *Tuesday* by David Wiesner. Jacket art copyright © 1991 by David Wiesner. Reprinted by permission of Clarion Books, an imprint of Houghton Mifflin Company. All rights reserved. Page 60–61: Illustration from *Tuesday* by David Wiesner. Copyright © 1991 by David Wiesner. Reprinted by permission of Clarion Books, an imprint of Houghton Mifflin Company. All rights reserved. Page 62: Jacket cover, from *The Three Pigs* by David Wiesner. Jacket illustrations copyright © 2001 by David Wiesner. Reprinted by permission of Clarion Books, an imprint of Houghton Mifflin Company. All rights reserved. Page 62–63: Illustration from *The Three Pigs* by David Wiesner. Copyright © 2001 by David Wiesner. Reprinted by permission of Clarion Books, an imprint of Houghton Mifflin Company. All rights reserved. Page 64: Jacket cover, from *Flotsam* by David Wiesner. Jacket illustrations copyright © 2006 by David Wiesner. Reprinted by permission of Clarion Books, an imprint of Houghton Mifflin Company. All rights reserved. Page 66: From *So What's It Like to Be a Cat?* by Karla Kuskin. Copyright © 2005 by Karla Kuskin (text); copyright © 2005 by Betsy Lewin (illustrations). By permission of Simon & Schuster. Page 67: Jacket cover, from *Click, Clack, Moo Cows That Type* by Doreen Cronin. Copyright © 2000 by Doreen Cronin (text); copyright © 2000 by Betsy Lewin (illustrations). By permission of Simon & Schuster. Page 68–69: From *Click, Clack, Moo Cows That Type* by Doreen Cronin. Copyright © 2000 by Doreen Cronin (text); copyright © 2000 by Betsy Lewin (illustrations). By permission of Simon & Schuster. Page 71: Jacket cover and excerpt, from *Hip, Hippo, Hooray!* by Betsy Lewin, copyright © 1982 by Betsy Lewin. Used by permission of Dodd Mead, A Division of Penguin Young Readers Group, A Member of Penguin Group (USA) Inc., New York, NY 10014. All rights reserved. Page 72: Jacket cover from *Cowgirl Kate and Cocoa*, by Erica Silverman, illustration copyright © 2005 by Betsy Lewin, reproduced by permission of Harcourt, Inc.

# INDEX